FULL DISCLOSURE
Seeking Truth After Sexual Betrayal

Volume One:
Understanding How a Disclosure Can Help You Heal

JANICE CAUDILL
PHD, CSAT-S, CCPS-S, PRT, SEP, IAT

DAN DRAKE
LMFT, LPCC, CCPS-S, CSAT-S

Independently Published: April 10, 2020
ISBN: 9798622559297

A Publication of Kintsugi Recovery Partners
www.KintsugiRecoveryPartners.com

PRAISE FOR
FULL DISCLOSURE:
SEEKING TRUTH AFTER SEXUAL BETRAYAL

I highly recommend this resource by Janice Caudill and Dan Drake for couples impacted by problematic sexual behavior/sex addiction and sexual betrayal. I believe the *Full Disclosure* workbooks will become one of the primary resources for couples who are seeking healing and for those who seek to assist them in that process.

> - Dr Barbara Steffens LPCC-S, BCC, CCPS,
> Assistant Professor Liberty University, Co-author of:
> *Your Sexually Addicted Spouse: How Partners Can Cope and Heal*

––––––––––––––––

Dr. Caudill and Drake present the most thorough discussion and practical guide on the process of disclosure to date in our field. This is a handbook for both clinician and client. The safety of the Partner and clarity for all involved is the best I have seen. A standard in our field has been born!

> - Douglas Weiss Ph.D., President of American Association for Sex Addiction Therapy
> Author of over 40 recovery and relationship books and
> 30 therapeutic DVDs, including *Helping Her Heal*

––––––––––––––––

One of the most challenging steps in navigating sexual betrayal is how to restore safety and the truth after ongoing lies and broken trust. For the couple, it's like sitting on a powder keg of tension and fear in the not knowing. The betrayer holds secrets fearing their partner will leave once they tell all. And devastated by what they've already discovered, the betrayed partner fears what they still don't know. *Full Disclosure: Seeking Truth After Sexual Betrayal* is finally here! Janice Caudill and Dan Drake have carefully diffused this process by offering practical steps and what we're looking for, hope after deception.

> - Sheri Keffer, Ph.D., Founder of Braveone.com and Author of:
> *Intimate Deception: Healing the Wounds of Sexual Betrayal*

Disclosure is often a misunderstood process. And sadly, huge mistakes have been made when disclosures were not prepared properly or facilitated by professionals who have the necessary expertise for this important process. As a result of those mistakes, partners who have already been wounded and betrayed by their spouse, are subjected to additional trauma.

Janice Caudill and Dan Drake have prepared a comprehensive work that helps partners understand the disclosure process, prepare for disclosure, and then guides them in how to move forward after the disclosure. if you are considering having a disclosure, or if you are a professional who wants to learn more about disclosures, this book will provide great insight.

- Dr. Milton Magness, Author of:
Thirty Days to Hope & Freedom from Sex Addiction
Stop Sex Addiction
Real Hope, True Freedom

Authors and clinicians Janice Caudill and Dan Drake have written one of the more comprehensive, hopeful, and sensitive books in Full Disclosure: Seeking Truth After Sexual Betrayal for couples who have experienced sexual betrayal due to sex addiction. It reassures the reader that they are not alone in the process and and it leaves no stone unturned in dealing with the complexities of this issue. Unique to Janice and Dan's approach is that they are able to weave the content together in such a way as to be sensitive to the the pain of the betrayed partner without shaming the addict. It is certain to become the manual that both clinicians and recovering individuals trust for the supportive guidance so needed in this journey.

- Kenneth M. Adams, Ph.D., CSAT-S, Author of:
Silently Seduced and *When He's Married to Mom*

Authors Janice Caudill and Dan Drake have created an essential guide and resource for couples whose relationship has been devastated by sexual betrayal. *Full Disclosure* is a comprehensive workbook for the disclosure process and a must-read before you begin the journey toward healing your relationship…. [They] have managed to create a workbook that is organized, healing and supportive, and a guiding light to those who are unable to see the path forward.

- Debra L. Kaplan, MA, MBA, LPC, CMAT, CSAT-S, Author of:
For Love and Money: Exploring Sexual & Financial Betrayal in Relationship

A formal disclosure is singlehandedly the most important process that a couple can use to rebuild the relationship once discovery has occurred. Janice Caudill and Dan Drake have written a comprehensive guide that I suspect will be considered "the bible" for couples who want to do this process. This step-by-step guide that will allow the Partner to know "the truth" in the least traumatizing format possible.

Professionals have been doing disclosures the wrong way for years and finally, clinicians, coaches, and clergy have a manual that they can learn from as it helps the couple recover from the impact of sexual betrayal. This is a much-needed resource written by two trusted and respected clinicians and educators in the field of sex addiction and Partner betrayal. I can't wait to pass this resource onto my clients!

- Carol Juergensen Sheets LCSW, CSAT, CCPS, PCC, Author of:
Help. Her. Heal: An Empathy Workbook for Sex Addicts to Help their Partner Heal

———————

Therapists are often faced with the responsibility of leading their client through the process of disclosing information about betrayal and other hurtful behaviors due to their addiction. Janice and Dan have done an exceptional job of developing a therapeutically sound curriculum that is written in a way which is supportive and non-shaming for both the addict and their partner. *Full Disclosure: Seeking Truth After Sexual Betrayal Volumes One, Two, and Three* are soon to be the "go to", "must have" books that every therapist will use while working through the disclosure process.

- Pennie J. Carnes, MA, LPC, CSAT, Co-Author of:
Shadows of the Cross: A Christian Companion to Facing the Shadow

———————

Full Disclosure provides a much-needed and long overdue resource in the fields of sex addiction and betrayal trauma recovery. The authors succeed at mapping out a disclosure process that is honoring of self-determination, mutually respectful of both parties, and clinically sound. I recommend this resource to any couple wanting to establish a solid foundation of truth and honesty in the wake of sexual betrayal.

- Jill Manning, Ph.D., CCPS, CCTP, Clinician, Researcher/Author, Public Speaker

Janice Caudill and Dan Drake have written an enormously helpful workbook explaining how to wisely and compassionately prepare clients to share the truth after sexual betrayal in a way that offers hope and healing to hurting couples. I wish all couples who have been affected by infidelity could have the kind of support this must-read guide offers.

- Laurie Hall, RScP, CPC, PSAP
President of APSATS, Author of:
An Affair of the Mind

————————

Janice Caudill and Dan Drake with amazing clarity, wisdom, respect, and compassion for the couple, take their readers through a carefully guided process of *Full Disclosure: Seeking Truth After Sexual Betrayal*. Theirs is the most comprehensive, Partner-sensitive disclosure workbook that will be used for years to come. Their depth of knowledge and experience treating sexual addiction and betrayal trauma serves to reassure and calm the natural disclosure fears of all involved. They passionately encourage and inspire confidence to journey through this difficult process, one step at a time. Those who brave disclosure with the expert guidance of Janice and Dan will benefit from their roadmap, and pathway to healing from the devastation and heartache of intimate betrayal. Ultimately, Full Disclosure can be the opportunity that you were hoping for, the first step towards transforming your relationship and moving towards greater intimacy and sexual healing.

- Dorit Reichental, MA, CSAT Candidate, CPC, ACC, ACC, Relational Recovery Coach, Founding Board Member of the Association of Partners of Sex Addicts Trauma Specialists

To all the brave women and men
seeking and sharing truth after sexual betrayal

TABLE OF CONTENTS

PREFACE

A note about language choices before we begin: We will be using the pronoun "we" throughout this workbook. "We" refers to us as the authors: Janice and Dan.

For sake of clarity, we will also be using the term "Partner" to refer to you, and "Discloser" to refer to the person who is doing the disclosing of sexual secrets. We will use the term "Partner" as a way of identifying you as the betrayed party and will address betrayal trauma from a Partner perspective. While we recognize that not all Partners experience trauma after sexual secrets are discovered or initially disclosed, we have found that the visceral feeling of betrayal is almost universal, and that a significant portion do experience betrayal trauma. In fact, Dr. Barbara Steffens' pioneering research found that 70% of the Partners in her study met criteria for posttraumatic stress disorder.[1]

At times, when writing sections for or about the "Discloser," we will also refer to him as "spouse." We are using this term to refer to anyone in a committed relationship and to avoid the confusion of using the same word (e.g., "Partner") to refer specifically to you and generically to your spouse.

We recognize that you may or may not conform to or identify with any gendered label and that your spouse likewise may or may not conform to or identify with any gendered label. In many cases we will use the gendered pronouns "she," "hers," or "her" to identify you and the gendered pronouns "he," "his," or "him" to identify the person sharing the disclosure.

We have only used these pronouns for the ease of reading, and in no way do we want to be insensitive or disrespectful to anyone's gender identity, nor do we assume that all seekers of truth are female or that sharers of truth are male. We hope you will substitute any pronouns that do not fit in your particular case for those that feel more appropriate for you.

We also want you to know that we are two among many professionals who are dedicated to making the professionally-guided disclosure process one that moves you toward healing. By sharing our approach, our aim is not to denigrate the procedures used by others. However, we do know how important it is to the outcome of your disclosure to be prepared properly by a qualified professional. It is our belief that each person, each relationship, is unique and so, too, will be each disclosure. Our intent is to demystify the process, inform you of your options, and provide resources for preparing so that you can design a disclosure for your unique needs. As such, this workbook is designed to be best used in conjunction with the Discloser's version for your spouse.

This workbook is a compilation of three separate volumes that cover the entire disclosure process. Volume One will help you better understand the Full Disclosure process and determine if it is right for you; Volume Two helps you create safety in the disclosure process by preparing you in heart, mind, body, and spirit; Volume Three will help you put yourself, and your relationship, back together after the Full Disclosure. This navigation of the healing process includes helping you make sense of what you learned in the disclosure and translating that into a Partner Impact Statement.

We also recognize that your individual situation is unique, and some issues you're going through may not have been addressed in this workbook. For example, we would have liked to address the issue of disclosure to children. However, that is a delicate subject, deserving of its own workbook, and is beyond the scope of preparing for disclosure from your spouse. We are aware that as yet, the majority of Partners seeking truth do not get the opportunity to participate in a professionally-guided disclosure because their spouse is not willing to provide that gift. We regularly hear the pain of those who have waited decades, and yet the aching need is still there. Our hope is that by providing resources for you and a step-by-step process for sharing truth in the Discloser's version of this workbook, a Full Disclosure of sexual betrayal becomes the norm.

Whatever your situation, we recommend that you work with your disclosure guide to fill in any gaps that you may need to address for your unique situation, in addition to what we've given you in this workbook. That brings up another important point: These workbooks are NOT intended to be used on your own without the support of a qualified professional. We've given you as much of a roadmap as possible to help you prepare for a disclosure, but this does not invalidate the need for disclosure guides to help you through this process. See Appendix 2 for more information on selecting a professional disclosure guide who can help.

This workbook contains information from a number of informal surveys to help clarify helpful points about the disclosure process. Be aware that these surveys have not been conducted under an Institutional Review Board, a process that ensures the study meets the rigorous standards of formal research. The survey outcomes may not be representative of the true population of Partners and Disclosers. Consequently, we have chosen to report only descriptive statistics and quotes from the participants who have given permission to share their words.

The Partners and Disclosers in these surveys participated in a professionally-led disclosure or fidelity polygraph about sexual betrayals that occurred in the context of sexually-addictive behavior. Although much of the workbook corresponds to this specific population, the process outlined is relevant for those dealing with betrayal for whom compulsivity is not the driving force. Both authors have used the process for disclosures of betrayals that do not involve addiction and have found these disclosures to be equally useful.

If you have already decided to do a disclosure, you may consider starting in Volume Two and then working back to Volume One as time permits. That way you can start preparing for disclosure as soon as possible while still considering this important information later. Volume Three helps navigate the healing process after the disclosure, including making sense of the information you learned in the disclosure and your Partner Impact Statement. Volume Three will then help you put yourself, and your relationship, back together after your disclosure.

Note that your workbook and your spouse's workbook, *Full Disclosure: How to Share the Truth after Sexual Betrayal*, have been designed to be used together. Some of the exercises in your workbook will correspond to exercises in your spouse's and vice versa. You will be working together to repair your relationship, whether preparing some tasks separately in your respective workbooks or other critical decision points together, such as designing the disclosure and coordinating boundary and coping plans. We hope these resources bring healing to you and to your relationship as you recover from the impact of sexual betrayal.

References:
[1]Steffens, B.(2005). The Effects of Disclosure on Wives of Sexual Addicts.
Unpublished dissertation, Regent University, Virginia Beach, VA.

FOREWORD

It is with the upmost respect, honor, delight (and many other superlatives!) that I highly recommend this resource by Janice Caudill and Dan Drake for couples impacted by problematic sexual behavior/sex addiction and sexual betrayal. I believe the *Full Disclosure* companion workbooks will become one of the primary resources for couples who are seeking healing and for those who seek to assist them in that process.

Once discovery or "D-Day" hits, couples are almost immediately hit with the prospect of having to share and receive painful information about previously withheld information. The betrayer fears telling all (If s/he knew me, s/he would leave me) and doesn't know how to begin to tell the truth. The betrayed partner fears both knowing the additional secrets and the possibility of not knowing it all (what else don't I know?). The betrayed partner knows that "not knowing" the truth has devastated them. Neither fully understand how to even begin the process in a way that leads toward healing.

How does this truth giving/receiving occur without adding even more pain and destruction into the relationship? Janice Caudill and Dan Drake are responding to just these questions in these resources. Years of experience, training, and more experience have led to a thoughtful, careful, and honoring process of intentional and "safe" telling and receiving truth.

Under the best of circumstances, this disclosure of previously unknown information (Formal, Therapeutic, or Full Disclosure) can be difficult for those who receive the information, and for those who are now revealing long-held secrets. Unfortunately, attempts to assist couples in this process have been too often experienced as harmful, especially for the one who is receiving this information. Therapists and other professionals did not have adequate training or resources to help couples navigate this difficult and painful journey. Couples had limited options for where and how to seek help.

The Association of Partners of Sex Addicts Trauma Specialists (APSATS) was formed to build on my research confirming posttraumatic stress in partners upon discovery of betrayal. The mission was to help train and prepare helping professionals to work with the betrayed partner using a trauma lens, the first organization to do so. Those of us involved in the formation of APSATS (which includes Janice Caudill and Dan Drake) received stories of how partners and couples were being treated by professionals. One of the most frequent complaints we heard in these stories centered on couples' experiences around the topic and process of disclosure. They told us of untrained professionals allowing this disclosure of information to occur in ways that brought further pain and trauma rather than relief and healing. We heard of partners being told they needed to wait for years to receive a disclosure, and too often heard partners say they were never offered disclosure of vital information needed for healing and decision-making. We heard of partners receiving disclosures with little to no preparation or support during the process. We heard of instances where there was no direction or assistance for the betrayer as he or she sought to share their sexual history. All of these types and instances of inadequate support and preparation needed to be corrected.

One of the main goals of APSATS is to provide excellent training to professionals so that they can offer ethical and appropriate support to their clients to avoid causing more harm to our clients. Harm or further injury was occurring to partners of "sex addicts" in large part due to un-trained or under-trained professionals attempting to facilitate this process of full disclosure. Janice Caudill and Dan Drake have been leaders in the sex addiction field, leaders in the Partner betrayal trauma field, leaders in the formation and growth of APSATS, and pioneers in helping to provide highly effective full disclosure processes for this population. They are now sharing all that they have learned along the way in a series of workbooks to assist both the betrayed Partner and the Discloser as they seek to obtain and share truth. It is my belief that their contributions to this process of "truth telling" will lead to hope and healing. In these workbooks, you will find tools, steps, guidelines, and support so that the process of full disclosure has the best opportunity to lead to healing.

I am so grateful to these colleagues and friends for their deep care and hope for couples seeking healing, which begins with knowing and being known. The *Full Disclosure* process is essential – and these resources will help you or those you help grow and heal with a foundation of truth and honesty.

Barbara Steffens, PhD, LPCC-S (Ohio), CCPS, CPC
Founding president APSATS (2012-2019), current member of the Board
Assistant Professor, Liberty University
Co-author of:
Your Sexually Addicted Spouse: How Partners Can Hope & Heal (Steffens & Means, 2009)

volume 1
The Full Disclosure Process

SECTION ONE:
THE EARTHQUAKE

It strikes without warning.

It strikes without warning. First there is a jolt, as if someone has hit the side of your house with a wrecking ball. Nothing breaks but you feel it. You sit up and look around, wondering "what just happened?" In the small hours of the morning, before light has begun to seep in and stain the day, the jolt awakens you to something. An approaching danger, something ominous. And then it happens. The earth begins to roar, a deafening, bone crushing sound, and then it begins to shake. The movement is violent, as if someone has picked up your house, turned it upside down and is shaking it to see what will come out. You duck into a doorway and hold on, waiting for it to stop.

The roar continues. The shaking seems interminable. You can hear everything inside being tossed into the middle where it breaks into a million pieces. Then, as suddenly as it starts, it stops. You're alive. It didn't kill you. Now you have to assess the damage in order to discover what can be salvaged, what can be repaired. As you let go of what you were holding onto, you realize you are shaking, too. The earthquake you have just experienced externally is also still jolting you inside, shaking your emotions, your trust and your faith. But you are still here. You think: "It couldn't have been that bad." Then there is a loud bang and the electricity goes out. You're in the dark, alone, feeling your way through the rubble of your life. And you wonder…

. . .What's next?

HEALING FROM SEXUAL BETRAYAL

We realize that nobody gets into a relationship hoping to use a workbook like this one. We're glad you have found this resource, but we wish your relationship had never been devastated by the impact of sexual betrayal in the first place.

That said, it is our belief that relationships can and do heal from sexual betrayal. We work with women and men each and every day who are healing after infidelity, who are thriving after battling sex addiction. So, if you are a brave woman or man taking the courageous steps toward healing, this workbook is for you.

You may have found this workbook for a variety of reasons, but we have created this resource primarily as a guide for you to come back into truth after betrayal. In the pages to come, we will detail a process for seeking truth about intimate deception, what you can expect, and how you can best prepare. By this, we are referring to a formal disclosure that is guided by a professional, preferably one with specific training and experience in helping you navigate a healing path for your relationship.

Before we detail this disclosure process, though, we thought it important to outline the nature of healing after sexual betrayal. You are at a vital point in your personal and relationship recovery. As you will see, the disclosure serves as a foundation for all work to come. Let's take a look at the overall healing journey from sexual betrayal and how a professionally-guided disclosure fits into this course.

When we enter a relationship, our ultimate goal is intimacy.

As humans, we have an innate need for connection and a desire to be known for who we are, to be seen for our authentic self, to attach in a healthy way. Sharing ourselves with authenticity, and the true desire for our loved ones to share their deepest selves with us, is intimacy, and it is the greatest achievement in our relationships. Intimacy involves many components, including choice, companionship, depth, shared vision, dreams of the future together, love, hope, faith, and mutual authenticity. Intimacy takes time to build, and it connects us to our closest loved ones. It is a zone that involves mutuality, give and take, communication, respect, and boundaries.

Intimacy requires vulnerability.

Intimacy requires vulnerability to develop, and vulnerability is an active process, where we share parts of ourselves, often the most hidden parts, with those closest to us. Note that in this workbook we are referring to vulnerability as an active choice, a step we willingly take in the quest for connection, as opposed to susceptibility to being harmed when choices are made for us without our consent. When we choose to be vulnerable, we take the risk to know and to be known at the deepest part of our core, and to experience the discomfort that comes with that effort. Without vulnerability, without sharing our hopes, dreams, fears, regrets, pains, and joys with another, we can't let ourselves be known by another or have the capacity to truly know another.

When we choose vulnerability, we build trust.

When we choose vulnerability, we build trust, and trust then invites further vulnerability to surface. We need to trust the person we are being vulnerable with – Can I share my full self without this information being exploited or without being rejected or abandoned? Can I trust that what is being shared is real? Can I respond with compassion without it being used to manipulate me, or without fear of the expectation that my pain should be over? Will I be given the time that it is going to take to be able to heal? Mutual trust allows vulnerability to thrive.

To allow trust and vulnerability to develop, we must feel safe.

To allow trust and vulnerability to develop, we must feel safe, physically and emotionally. Safety is the fertile soil that allows trust to flourish, and when safety, trust, and vulnerability continue to build on each other, intimacy can deepen in a relationship.

We must have truth.

Ultimately, to provide a context for safety to develop, we must have truth. Most of us enter into relationships with the expectation of truth. We assume that our loved ones are who they say they are, that they are presenting us with true and accurate information. When we see things that are contradictory to the truth we know, we give our loved ones the benefit of the doubt because we choose to have trust in them. We don't assume that they are hiding themselves or their behaviors from us when we have truth and honesty in a relationship. Just the opposite – we assume their truthfulness. Truth, then, becomes a foundation upon which safety, trust, vulnerability, and intimacy are built.

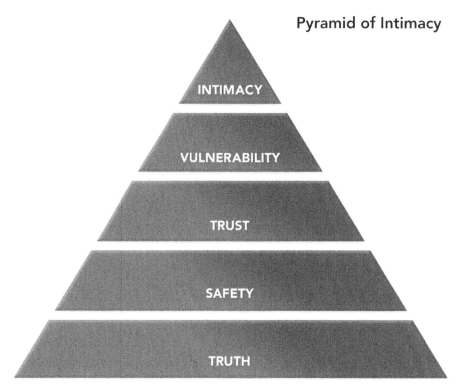

Pyramid of Intimacy

INTIMACY

VULNERABILITY

TRUST

SAFETY

TRUTH

Figure 1

The pyramid we just described looks like Figure 1 above.

As you can see, intimacy, or healthy attachment, is the highest point on this pyramid. It is built on a foundation of vulnerability, trust, safety, and ultimately, truth. With these components, relationships flourish in love and health. They are satisfying and attached in a healthy way.

Unfortunately, when couples are devastated by sexual betrayal, it is not just their intimacy that suffers; it is the whole pyramid that crumbles, starting with the foundation of truth. The relationship you thought you were building for weeks, months, years, or even decades shatters when lies and sexual secrets are discovered. Discovery is so devastating because it destroys the truth that served as a foundation to your relationship. Said another way, "Relational traumas, often called attachment injuries, occur when one person betrays, abandons or refuses to provide support for another with whom he or she has developed an attachment bond."[2] This trauma is exactly what occurs after sexual betrayal. It happens to both you and your relationship.

Looking back at the pyramid, if the foundation of truth crumbles, then safety erodes in the relationship. Without safety, trust dies, and without trust, vulnerability becomes locked behind protected walls. Without vulnerability, intimacy withers. So, we can see why so many betrayed Partners refer to the day of discovery as "D Day" – this was the day that the world as they knew it crumbled.

So how do we heal in light of this devastation? Most Partners recognize over time that the old relationship is gone and can never be built again. We can't just "move on" and rebuild the old pyramid because it was fraught with a lack of truth, safety, and authenticity. In fact, if the pain that results from betrayal is dismissed and the damage ignored without your spouse taking action to help restore a sense of safety in the relationship, you will feel a perpetual sense of threat *(Steffens and Means, 2009)*.[3] The journey of healing through sexual betrayal will involve sifting through the rubble of the original pyramid and building a new one in its place – a pyramid that involves trust and safety. The first thing that will have to be built is a new foundation, which is one of truth. We have found the best way to establish a new foundation based on truth for couples impacted by sexual betrayal comes through a full disclosure of the transgressions. Knowing the full extent of the damage allows couples to more fully repair the foundation in their relationship.

We wish you and your relationship nothing but the best. We want you to make it through this process. We want you to develop a new intimate relationship that has vulnerability, trust, safety, and a connection like you may never have had before. We absolutely think this is possible, but it will have to be erected with a new foundation based on truth.

Full disclosure of sexual betrayal is a way of building a new foundation to your relationship, one that cultivates intimacy and love. In the pages that follow, we will describe a process for creating this new foundation of truth. We want to help you develop a safe disclosure that allows for a full accounting of the truth so that you can establish as strong a foundation as possible to the new relationship that will evolve.

References:
[2]*Steffens, B. & Means, M. (2009).* Your Sexually Addicted Spouse: How partners can cope and heal. *Far Hills, NJ: New Horizon Press. P. 11.*
[3]*Ibid.*

SECTION TWO:
THE DISCLOSURE PROCESS

WHAT IS A FULL DISCLOSURE?

Now that we have talked about the importance of rebuilding a new foundation of truth in your relationship, let's explore further: what IS a disclosure?

Chances are, if you're reading this book you have already experienced at least one disclosure, one that was most likely not guided by a professional. Most early disclosures after initial discovery of sexual betrayal are a series of staggered confessions, usually forced by circumstances, most often with you discovering evidence of deceit, and then pressing your spouse for information. Even more frequently the betraying party shares some information without divulging all of the violations of trust. These staggered confessions are painful and will continue to re-traumatize the relationship. Dr. Milton Magness says, "A disclosure that is less than 100 percent honest is not a disclosure but a deception."[4] Because of this, what we have found most helpful for relationships in rebuilding trust through truth, honesty, accountability, and transparency is a **Full Disclosure.**

A Full Disclosure is a facilitated process, usually led by trained professionals who can help couples get to a level playing field of truth. In a FD (for simplicity, at times we will be using the abbreviation "FD" for "Full Disclosure"), the shards of reality that have been fragmented at discovery are now laid out on the table to be re-assembled. Like putting a puzzle together, FDs place all the disclosure pieces on the table, and the lies are replaced with honesty so the greater truth can be put together. It is from this foundation of truth and honesty that your relationship can begin to rebuild.

There is no official, universal title for a planned, Full Disclosure. It may be called different names by different professionals, such as a professionally-guided disclosure, formal disclosure, therapeutic disclosure, or a full or facilitated therapeutic disclosure. For the purposes of this workbook, we are referring to this process of preparation as a Full Disclosure that culminates in the Rite of Truth, a passage of truth restoration. The purpose of a FD is to restore a foundation of truth. Hence, we are considering the session where your spouse shares and you receive this full truth as a "Rite of Truth." At times we'll use the term "Truth Rite" or "Rite." We wanted to set apart this session, marking its significance in the building of a new foundation for you and for your relationship: A foundation that is now based upon full and complete truth. Regardless of the name, it is important that you understand what the process involves and what it does not.

First, what a Full Disclosure is NOT:

- FD is not a bomb that your spouse drops on your relationship with no careful preparation on his part and zero awareness by you that it is coming. This blindsides you, which never helps with making sense of bad news. It also replicates what may have happened for you in the initial discovery, making it much harder for this type of disclosure to be part of repairing the trust foundation.

- It is not a detailing of exploits. Providing every single detail of sexual encounters creates mental pictures that become the source of intrusive thoughts and nightmares that impede your healing. This can be especially traumatizing if you were not requesting this level of information.

- A FD is not the information that is shared only when you ask the perfectly phrased question that leaves no loopholes. That is not a disclosure; it is a confession and it puts you in the position of having to cross-examine your spouse to get to the facts about what has happened. Information gained in this way will not build a lasting foundation, even if the full truth comes out.

- A FD does not require you to set truth traps by asking questions you already know the answers to in order to assess how forthcoming your spouse will be. In these cases, he may only admit to the behaviors he believes you already know. Prioritizing the protection of his secrets in lieu of repairing trust is not a Full Disclosure.

- It is not the fruit of your questioning process that begins at bedtime and lasts into the wee hours of the morning. Truth extraction techniques might be effective, but any disclosure that results from the same methods the FBI might also use negates the development of trust.

- A disclosure is not about punishment, nor is it for either party to exert power or control over the other. The process of seeking truth can absolutely be empowering, but it is not meant as a form of disempowering one party at the expense of the other.

So, what IS a Full Disclosure?

A Full Disclosure is a structured process, frequently facilitated by trained professionals. FDs vary based upon what each individual couple and Partner needs, but generally they include a full history of your spouse's sexual acting-out behaviors. Sometimes these disclosures include history prior to the relationship, and other times they describe behaviors since the relationship began. We leave this decision up to you, depending on what information will help you to begin to make sense of your world that just shattered. A FD shines a light into the darkness, helping couples reset from a foundation of truth. A FD measures the extent of your spouse's betrayal behaviors and, ultimately, the extent of the damage those behaviors have caused to you and your relationship.

Every disclosure that we facilitate is personalized to each couple, since the needs of each couple are so unique. This workbook is a resource to help you create the optimal disclosure that fits for YOU. FDs are done best when they involve preparation for everyone. The clearer you can be about your expectations, goals, and what the process involves, the more the FD will give you the help you're looking for. We cannot emphasize enough how important it is for you to find a trained professional to help guide you through this process, as we have found that FDs done poorly can only add to the suffering you are experiencing in your relationship. There will be pain regardless, but an experienced, trained guide can help it be the type of pain that is inevitable in cleaning out the wound so that deeper healing can begin. We will provide some considerations in the pages to come about selecting a good disclosure guide for your unique situation.

While each disclosure differs based on your needs as a couple, we generally have found the following guidelines to make Full Disclosures the most successful:

- You and your spouse will BOTH need adequate preparation. This process is not just about your spouse unloading his story. He will need someone who can challenge him about truth, help him write out his disclosure document, prepare him for the FD, and to help guide him during and after the process. YOU will need someone who can help you clarify expectations, determine your healing needs, and who can help prepare you physically, mentally and emotionally before, during, and after the Rite of Truth. You will also need someone who can help you formulate what types of information you need in the disclosure and the most effective means of seeking that information. As a couple, you will need professionals who understand the impact that the betrayal has had on your intimacy pyramid and use the FD as a critical tool for healing the relationship.

- It is important that you are given as much choice as possible in this process. Choices, knowledge, and having a voice were taken from you through your spouse's sexual betrayals. A FD is a chance to regain some sense of stability again. The Discloser version of this workbook emphasizes that the more support your spouse shows you in this process, the deeper the foundation of safety will become in the relationship. The more he gives you honesty, openness, and empathy, the quicker you will be able to heal.

- Disclosures should be mediated by at least one trained professional. It is helpful to have both your spouse's and your guide in the Rite of Truth if possible. At the very least, the space needs to be a safe place to process the information.

- Understand and explore the benefits and risks of doing a FD at this time with your disclosure guide team before doing a disclosure. The more information you can glean about realistic expectations, the better your disclosure outcome will be.

- Make sure to have a good plan before, during, and after your disclosure. Avoid intensely stressful times at work or important dates (such as birthdays or holidays) that you won't want tarnished by memories of the FD. Work with your guides on thinking through all the factors that go into a good plan. Using the exercises in this workbook will go a long way to helping you and your guides customize a FD plan that works for your circumstances.

Ultimately, you want to find a safe place where you can get the information needed to help your relationship move forward without being re-traumatized by learning more of the "gory details" than necessary. The FD is a place to know the extent of the behaviors to begin regaining footing, rather than examining the minute details of every acting-out event.

DISCLOSURE MISCONCEPTIONS

Now that we have talked about what a Full Disclosure is and what it is not, we need to dispel some common misconceptions that couples have about disclosures.

COMMON *GENERAL* MISCONCEPTIONS ABOUT DISCLOSURE:

Misconception 1: We can only do a Full Disclosure when my spouse and I are completely grounded and he has at least 90 days of continued sobriety.

Of course, we absolutely recommend that you both are as grounded as possible, and that you both will have built up the best internal and external resources you possibly can prior to disclosure. In fact, this kind of resourcing and preparation will be a point of focus in this workbook. We also advocate for continued sobriety on your spouse's part, since further relapses can be devastating to the trust being rebuilt. We recognize that preparing for your Rite of Truth can take a substantial period of time, especially if you are creating the type of written disclosure document as we're laying out here: at least 6 to 8 weeks, or more if the guide does not help edit on a fee for time basis outside of scheduled sessions.

The benefit of waiting longer for a disclosure is that you will have more time to come out of the initial shock of the discovery and your spouse will have more time to get out of the "fog" his sexual behaviors put him in. This will allow him to better recall and integrate information he has likely spent years working hard to deny, minimize, avoid, dissociate from, or compartmentalize. Moreover, according to Dr. Jill Manning, "neuroscience research supports the idea that periods of abstinence from addictive processes can physiologically help the brain heal and thereby improve cognitive functioning and recall of past events, which in turn benefits Partners who are seeking quality answers to important questions."[5] Periods of sobriety prior to the disclosure may also provide you more time to learn how to ground, identify safe supports, clarify disclosure needs, and emotionally prepare for the disclosure.

That said, if we look back at the pyramid of intimacy we talked about previously, you can see that safety is built on a foundation of truth. So, you may find that you can never fully be grounded or safe UNTIL you have had disclosure. In medical terms, if something is ailing our body, we would never want to begin treatment without knowing the extent of the problem. Instead, the first step we need to go through is getting an accurate diagnosis. Similarly, for us, the disclosure process after sexual betrayal is a way that we get a clearer picture of the extent of the problem. It is the equivalent of a set of X-rays in that it is understanding the extent of the problem from which we build our healing journey after sexual betrayal.

While we would advocate for your spouse's establishing and sustaining sobriety before disclosure, we also need to look realistically at how long this will take. The commonly recommended ninety-day period, for example, may be a long time for you to wait when it could take him so much longer than that, considering the wait for him to get into recovery, find a sponsor, and build continued sobriety. Some people in recovery can take months or even years to establish consistent sobriety, and we have also found that some individuals only gain sobriety AFTER the FD.

Consequently, you may need to consider whether the damage from waiting may outweigh the damage of going ahead with a FD. A survey of Partners' experiences of the recovery process conducted by the Association of Partners of Sex Addicts Trauma Specialists (APSATS) suggests the prolonged wait time between the discovery of betrayal and the full disclosure can be more distressing than the FD itself in some cases. On a 10-point scale of emotional distress, with a "10" indicating the highest level of emotional distress, discovery, wait time, and FD distress were rated as 9.6, 9.2 and 7.7, respectively. We can see this distress comparison depicted in Figure 2:[6]

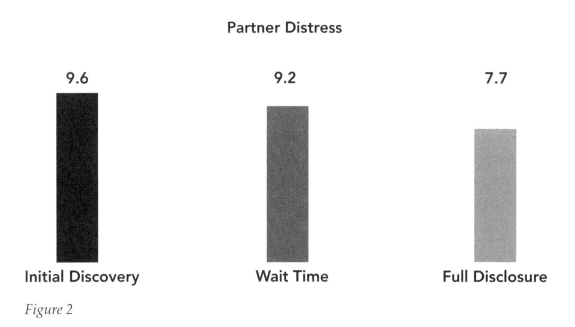

Partner Distress

Figure 2

So, you can see that the respondents to the survey found the prolonged time they spent waiting for disclosure MORE distressing than the actual FD. Please do talk to your guide based on your unique situation regarding the amount of time that would be best for you to wait for disclosure, particularly if you are dealing with any medical or mental health issues or your spouse's issues with establishing or maintaining sobriety, in addition to preparing for this disclosure.

Misconception 2: The disclosure can be effectively done in a 50-minute therapy hour by joining my spouse's session

Therapists, coaches, clergy, or other guides who are untrained or inexperienced in guiding full disclosures may think that there are only one or two issues that your spouse needs to share with you or that you shouldn't be allowed to ask questions that help clarify what happened, which can be done in a typical therapeutic or professional setting. This might be possible for a partial disclosure but is not the case for a Full Disclosure. Equally of concern are professionals who parcel out the FD across a span of days or multiple weekly sessions to suit their own needs instead of the needs of their client. Imagine if a surgeon stopped in mid-surgery because, "Your time is up for today. My next patient is waiting."

As you will see in the later parts of this workbook, you and your spouse will each have a lot of important work to do in preparation for your Rite of Truth. Each of you doing your work on the front end will better help you minimize further disclosures down the road from only partial truths being shared. Also, doing this preparation will minimize the traumatic impact that disclosure may have on you. We have found that good preparation can prevent a lot of the damage that poorly prepared FDs can create. This preparation may look different depending on the setting you choose for your Rite of Truth: with your therapist in their private practice office, with a clergy member, with a professional coach, or in an intensive or treatment center setting. Regardless of the setting, as you'll see in the pages of this book, adequate preparation is crucial for the success of your Rite of Truth and your overall FD process.

———————

COMMON MISCONCEPTIONS *YOU* MAY HAVE ABOUT DISCLOSURE:

Misconception 1: My spouse is the one with the problem, I don't need my own support in preparing for the disclosure.

We absolutely agree that your spouse is the one who brought the problem to you and your relationship. You didn't cause it and you can't control it. And he does need support in preparing for the FD.

That said, as you'll see in this workbook and Volumes Two and Three that follow, there are a lot of areas where you will need support going through this process as well. From building resources outside and inside of yourself to helping shape the way the Rite of Truth plays out, you'll have a lot of preparation work to do. We do understand how hard it may be to do this.

One analogy we often find helpful to think about is that of getting into a car accident. Imagine you were driving, obeying the speed limit and all the laws. All of a sudden, you get rear-ended by the car behind you. Through no fault of your own, your car is damaged and you sustain injuries. You have to complete a police report, deal with insurance companies to fix your car, and, most importantly, get help for the injuries you sustained in the accident, including a possible hospital stay. You may even require ongoing physical therapy or other medical procedures in the future. Again, through no fault of your own, you may still require medical attention for a period of time after this accident.

Even though you are not at fault, the decision about whether to cooperate with the ongoing medical treatment and physical therapy is yours to make. While that physical therapy may expose you to some degree of pain as you work through your injuries, if you want to regain lost function, you have to be willing to show up multiple times a week and struggle through discomfort for the next several months. Regardless of how the injury occurred, your healing will require you to be an active participant in your own recovery process.

Similarly, though you didn't cause the sexual betrayal you've experienced, you have been impacted by it. You've sustained injuries from betrayal trauma and require support to make it through this journey. That's why you need to seek support in preparing for this FD, and your disclosure guide can be an integral part of that support.

Misconception 2: I have so many questions – I need him to answer everything! (I need to know EVERYTHING about his past).

Although we understand the desire to learn everything, we know that some information is much more vital than others, and we want to help you focus on what will be most necessary for you in establishing that foundation of truth. We will talk more later about emotionally-focused and emotionally-driven questions of the heart as opposed to clarifying and fact-focused questions. Know that you will have an opportunity to think about all the questions you need your spouse to answer concerning his past sexual activities. This book and your disclosure guide can help you determine which of these questions are emotionally-focused questions to address further after the FD in contrast to fact-focused, content questions to address in the FD. For example, wanting to know all the details about "the other woman" in terms of body type, hair, etc. may be about a deeper question of, "Do you love me?" or "Was I not enough?" Clarifying questions help you better understand specifics of your spouse's behavior, the facts of that behavior, such as, "On _____, when you told me _____, were you using that time to go do _____?" These questions give you the puzzle pieces that help you to determine truth, see the bigger patterns, and to validate your intuition.

This FD is your opportunity to hear all the facts. After the FD, ongoing recovery work will help you process the pain of the betrayal – your emotionally-focused questions will help guide your journey of grief. That's when you'll bring in your questions of the heart. We'll talk about this more in Volume Two, but future healing work you can do as a couple will involve both validation of fact-focused questions and emotionally-focused heart questions.

Misconception 3: It doesn't take long to write the disclosure.
We recognize that there are a lot of different ways to facilitate a disclosure process. As you'll see in the pages of these workbooks, there is a lot of work to do for both you and your spouse to prepare for the disclosure.

Note from the authors: It generally takes us a minimum of 6-8+ weeks to prepare a disclosure document with an outpatient client, with multiple revisions of the document along the way. And this is with a client who is motivated, working diligently, not distracted by escalating episodes of distress between the two of you, and in some cases with much of the review by the guide happening outside of the scheduled sessions. Our job as disclosure guides is to help your spouse take a hard, truthful look at his own history, to give you all the information you need from the FD, and to help him present it in a way that is as safe for you as possible (not defensive, justifying, blaming, etc.). Preparing the disclosure document is sometimes the experience that finally breaks through denial and allows your spouse to see the depth of destruction his behavior has caused. This can be a powerful emotional process with aftershocks of awareness. As you can see, creating the document is more complicated than simply sitting down and writing it.

We understand that some have crafted approaches to FD where they can prepare the disclosure document in a day or weekend. Those can be effective depending on what you're needing, if you are willing to sacrifice a little quality to speed up the process, or if you're willing to do some preparation work beforehand and buckle down and work with sustained intensity. However, the multiple exercises in your spouse's version of Volume Two of his workbook attest that there are a lot of components to preparing the most effective disclosure document possible. We encourage those of you planning to use an intensive option for a FD to use the exercises included in these workbooks to prepare for your disclosure intensive. Adding preparation prior to your intensive will enable you both to dig deeper and experience a higher-quality disclosure.

Misconception 4: I have no prep work to do. My only job is to wait for the disclosure.
You have the choice to do no prep work for the disclosure, but we see two problems in taking a passive stance. First, by taking this position, your behavior communicates that your spouse can set a low bar for thoroughness in his disclosure. Our experience suggests that when given the option to use a lower standard, most people will. If you need relatively little

information disclosed to you, then this won't be a problem. If, however, you need more than the bare minimum, there will probably be a gap between the questions you need answered for your own peace of mind and what will be provided if your own preparation behavior communicates "low bar."

If you have suspicions that are going to haunt you if not included, we encourage you to develop questions that need to be addressed by the FD. Just as preparing a list of questions about medical issues increases the chance you will remember to ask for answers in your next medical appointment, your needs are more likely to be met if you work with your disclosure guide to develop questions for your Rite of Truth as well.

Secondly, compared to prior discoveries, this time you know in advance that painful information is coming; this time you can use that early warning to prepare and come through it in better shape. If you know a bad storm is coming, common sense says to prepare so you can better ride out the storm. In a FD, what you have to prepare is YOU. This workbook series is designed to help you focus your needs and compose your questions, as well as prepare you to withstand the storm and come out stronger in the end.

Misconception 5: My only prep work is to prepare questions for disclosure.

It is true that a major component of your FD preparation will involve the generation of specific questions, but preparing questions is only one part of your preparation. A significant component of preparing for disclosure is helping you build new coping resources, a "coping cup," and a team of resources around you.

In this workbook series, we have provided one path you may take for your FD, which includes both preparation for the content (e.g., your questions) and emotional and behavioral preparation (e.g., healthy coping behavior choices).

Misconception 6: I need my spouse to FEEL MY PAIN for this disclosure to be effective.

We absolutely agree that he needs to be present with you and hold space for your pain during the FD. In a perfect world he would also be able to feel your pain during the Rite. His workbook and disclosure guide will help him work on developing empathy and an understanding of what you're going through. That's a vital part of his long-term recovery as well as your long-term healing in the relationship.

However, because your FD may well be taking place early on in your healing journey, your spouse may not yet have learned empathy for your pain. So, he may not be able to feel your pain with you during the preparations or the Rite of Truth. While it may be difficult for you for him to not feel your pain yet, and we do acknowledge that it is his long-term work to do, it will reflect where he is at in his emotional maturity. Emotional maturity is something that develops over time in recovery. Being able to hold your pain and grieve with you is a vital piece of his work to help you heal in the future.

For the present disclosure, though, the focus is on you receiving all the information you need to make informed choices about your future. The FD levels the "knowing field" which in turn re-balances the distribution of power in your relationship. We believe that this disclosure can be effective even if your spouse has not fully learned the language of empathy. Know that he will be instructed to NOT blame shift, get defensive, shut down in shame, etc. He will be working with his guide on these things in the FD, and his ongoing work will be to hold you in your pain. Additionally, his work going forward will be to take full responsibility for his actions, to develop empathy for your pain, and to be there for you in your grieving process. Much of his work post-disclosure will be twofold: to maintain a solid program of recovery and to help heal your relationship by bolstering intimacy deficits.

Misconception 7: If my spouse gets defensive or goes into shame during the Rite of Truth, it is a failure.

Your spouse will be working on attuning to your heart in the Rite of Truth, as opposed to getting defensive or collapsing in shame. That is part of his work to prepare for the FD. Yet we find that many Disclosers do go into shame or defensiveness in the FD. That's why we recommend disclosure guides to help support you and to help keep your spouse focused on you while taking responsibility for his actions. *How* he responds to sharing his history is also valuable information. It tells you something about his emotional maturity. Sometimes a FD shows you that he is developing that maturity, other times it reveals the work that needs to follow the FD.

Your spouse may get defensive or spiral in shame, but this doesn't mean your disclosure is a waste. It just means that defensiveness and shame is the truth of where he is at in his recovery. If your spouse is able to bounce back and deliver the information to you, he is showing you how he puts his recovery tools in motion. In these cases, we have found that disclosures can still be effective.

Misconception 8: Once we finish this disclosure, I will have every piece of information about my spouse's past sexual behaviors.

The goal of the FD process is to give you all the facts that you need about your spouse's past to move forward. He will be doing a lot of work to give you all of this information. That said, most Disclosers we have worked with going through a FD tend to compartmentalize information. They've blocked out painful memories or live in different compartments – work, family, relationship, etc. As much as we will help him open up those compartments to give you a complete disclosure, sometimes the Rite of Truth is what helps those compartments to start opening up. Consequently, it is possible that, as he does future work following the FD, it may open up even more compartmentalized memories. That does not necessarily mean that he was intentionally lying or withholding information during the FD; it is just the way compartmentalized memories work.

It is possible that additional information about historical events may come to light after you go through the FD process. This workbook will emphasize along the way that your spouse's work is to come into truth rather than intentionally hold back or lie about the past, so that the FD you will receive is true and complete to the best of his knowledge. The FD represents his memory of the facts, which his guide will work on making as full and truthful as it possibly can be. The goal is to clear away any and all betrayal lies and fill in the gaps about information that was withheld from you.

Additional information coming to light after FD doesn't invalidate the whole disclosure process. We recognize that it can be destabilizing to the fragile foundation of trust you're building in the relationship should additional information about past betrayals come to light. However, additional information that is excavated from the past after the Rite of Truth is different than information that was intentionally withheld or lied about. Each of your Volume Two preparing for FD workbooks will contain a boundary exercise so you both agree on what the standard operating procedure will be should information be remembered after the Rite.

Misconception 9: There will be no more lies after the disclosure.

We hear over and over from Partners some variation of, "I can handle the truth, I just can't handle more lies." Lies, deception, withholding, and manipulation are incredibly devastating to your relationship. In fact, we often find that when relationships aren't able to transcend the damage created by the betrayal, it is more often because of continued lies and deceptions rather than the history of sexual behaviors.

Our hope for you is that there will be no more lies after the disclosure. The corresponding workbook for your spouse emphasizes that continued lies and deception will erode, if not destroy, the foundation he is trying to build through the FD. He will be encouraged to work to build a new foundation of honesty; if he recognizes that he has told a lie or deceived you, circling back and owning that lie generally goes better in relationships than having you eventually find out about it or have to ask, "Is there anything you need to tell me?"

It is probable that your spouse will be in the process of learning a new way of walking in integrity through truth. He will probably stumble some along the way, so he may lie post-disclosure, not always about acting-out behaviors. However, our expectation is that these lies become fewer and fewer, that they're volunteered rather than discovered, and that truth is increasingly accompanied by empathy and remorse rather than defensiveness or blame.

Misconception 10: I will be expected to forgive all at the end of the Rite of Truth or we won't be able to move forward.

The if or when of forgiveness is a personal decision. Although we don't expect it, we hope that someday you can forgive, because forgiveness would mean you have come to acceptance of the past and it is no longer haunting you. However, we caution you not to grant forgiveness prematurely or out of a sense of obligation. Your role in the Rite of Truth is to focus on what the facts are. As much as you may want to put all the puzzle pieces together and understand what the big picture of those facts is, we rarely see this happen during the Rite itself, unless your disclosure takes place after you are deep into the recovery process. For most, understanding won't come until you have spent some time wrapping your brain around the facts that are provided and what they mean to you. Forgiveness that comes before understanding is usually premature and can become an impediment to healing.

We discourage you from forgiving out of a sense of obligation or duty. When you have a greater understanding of what was disclosed means to you, you may discover a hidden betrayal from your spouse if he manipulated you into forgiving by pushing you to feel a sense of obligation or guilt. Some Partners also experience a subtle pressure to forgive from their faith community, family, recovery community, or even recovery guides. It is important that there be no hidden agendas for you in the disclosure process. If this has been part of your experience, we encourage you to give yourself all the time you need AFTER the Rite to come to your own decision on forgiveness.

COMMON MISCONCEPTIONS *YOUR SPOUSE* MAY HAVE ABOUT THE PROCESS:

It is important for you to be aware of the misconceptions and fears your spouse may have about FD. It was also important for the authors to be transparent about how those misconceptions are handled in his companion workbook.

Below are 10 common misconceptions that your spouse may have about FD, taken directly from the Discloser's companion workbook. We have included them here as they appear in his book so you can see some typical ways he may wrestle with this FD process.

Please look through these to see if any of these resonate with what your spouse has been expressing about FD. We have opted to keep these misconceptions written from your spouse's perspective, to better help you recognize and respond to his voice if any of these misconceptions fit his experience.

Discloser Misconception 1: Sharing all of my sexual secrets will destroy the relationship (i.e., why would she stay after I share all of this)?

This is a common misconception held by most of those giving the disclosure. If you are expressing this sentiment, we usually find this belief stemming from much earlier core beliefs about yourself, others, and the world. For example, many commonly held beliefs from those going through this disclosure process include, "I'm bad," "I'm unworthy," "I'm not enough," "I'm defective," "I'm a fraud," etc. As a way of coping with these beliefs, many of us can begin to hide parts of ourselves from others, for if we hide our defects from others then we can still receive love, care, and support. So, we develop assumptions. "If she knew everything about me, she'd reject me," or "It will never be enough for her." And, of course, when the bad, shameful parts of ourselves include actions that are harmful to the person we care about, we want to hide them all the more.

So, you can see how sharing all your sexual secrets with your Partner would cut to the core of these beliefs about your worthiness, lovability, etc. And in fact, it MAY be true that the information you share in this disclosure is too much for your Partner to bear. Some pieces may have been too much. Yet what we find in nearly all cases is the opposite. We regularly hear Partners saying a variation of, "I can handle the truth, but what I can't handle are continued lies."

It is less likely that the information you SHARE will kill the relationship. Instead, it is more likely that, when your Partner discovers more lies, manipulations, deceit, these continued discoveries will be what kills the relationship. We have found that it is the process of Partners starting to rebuild trust based on perceived truth, only to have that foundation continue to be eroded, that ultimately destroys relationships, as opposed to the actual information you share.

Discloser Misconception 2: I have already told her everything – Why do we need to go through a Full Disclosure?

On the flipside of the previous misconception, we often hear from the disclosing party that they've told their Partner "everything." So, if they have already told everything, what's the point in going through with a FD? This is a good question that we need to carefully consider. First, this process is more than just about the information you share with your Partner. For example, if you believe you've shared everything with your Partner, HOW did you share it with her? Did you share it after carefully considering every word you'd be sharing? Did you share it in a way that honored her safety? Did you share the information without defensiveness or collapsing into shame? Did you share it all at one time? Did you do a detailed reflection into your past to make sure you didn't forget something? And think carefully – did you REALLY share EVERYTHING with your Partner?

In our experience, you may have shared the main categories of behaviors you've engaged in. That said, the information shared often is lacking in detail (or may have been shared with too much detail). We have also found that this information is commonly shared in bits in pieces, as a result of long, drawn-out arguments or confessionals, and the information is rarely given with careful consideration of the wording AND delivery.

For this reason, the Rite of Truth is a way that you share all of this information in one setting. In the best-case scenario, you HAVE shared everything with your Partner! If that is the case, this process will go more smoothly for you, and the Rite of Truth will perhaps even be relieving for your Partner. So, you get the added benefit of having your Partner see that you're willing to do what she needs to feel safe by going through the FD. This will only enhance the trust and safety you are rebuilding post-discovery. The FD process also better enables your Partner to assimilate the information you are sharing with her. Conversely, information shared over a prolonged period of time may feel to her like having multiple "partial surgeries" to fix a medical problem. Rarely is this successful or without unnecessary pain. As a result, she may not have been able to take in or retain all that you shared with her. Doing a FD will better enable her to hear and retain the information you're sharing, to better help you establish a new foundation from which to heal.

Misconception 3: I can do this on my own. I don't need professionals to help me prepare or to guide me.

We absolutely recognize that nobody's first choice is to go through this disclosure process, let alone have to share this information with other people, even those who are professionally prepared to handle such information. It can be scary to share this information with ANYONE. In fact, that is usually one of the reasons most people hide this information in the first place: because it's shameful.

That said, you may have already seen what has happened when you tried to confess or disclose on your own. Most people share partial truths, create additional lies, stagger information, or disclose in a less-than-helpful manner. That's where a professional disclosure guide comes in: They have experience navigating this process and can help you with your own relational healing. They will guide you through writing your disclosure and be your support during the Rite of Truth. This is such a complicated process, which is why we have written these workbooks. We find that most couples need professional support to help them know what information to request or to share, as well as how to best go through the Rite of Truth. You wouldn't rely on yourself to remove a cancerous tumor from your body. Similarly, let an experienced professional disclosure guide help you and your Partner navigate this disclosure. Their job is not to shame you, but to rather help you to share truth so that your Partner, you, and your relationship can heal.

Discloser Misconception 4: Once I complete this disclosure, we can get back to the relationship we had (i.e., now she will finally "get over it")

Recovery is a process of grief. Most Partners intuitively know after discovery that they no longer have the relationship they once had. Like an earthquake that has demolished a house, there is no going back to the "old house" after it is been bulldozed. A new home, and an even more beautiful one in our opinion, can be built. Though the house will never be the same as it was in the past, it can still be transformed into something beautiful.

You need to know that although you ARE giving her what she needs to heal by going through FD, you won't be able to go back to your previous relationship before "D-Day." In fact, many Partners mark time from "before D-Day" to "after D-Day."

Because recovery is a process of grief, you also need to know that grief is a process. It doesn't happen once. You may be able to compartmentalize pain or memories, but your Partner may not. Healing from betrayal trauma and its associated grief takes time, patience, and will involve you stepping into your Partner's pain. Your Partner will almost certainly have more questions over time, even after your FD. Again, this is the way she can integrate the pain of the grief process. Typically, we find the questions shifting more from content-oriented questions, (e.g., who, what, when, where) questions to more process questions (e.g., how, why). These questions help your Partner process the pain she has experienced, and you joining alongside her will better enable (and also speed up) the healing process.

Discloser Misconception 5: This only affects us, not others around us

Sometimes it is the case that your sexual behaviors only affected yourself and your Partner. Yet, for many going through the disclosure process, your behaviors have had an impact on family members, work colleagues, as well as intersecting with places and events that are part of your Partner's world. For example, if your sexual acting out occurred in a favorite restaurant or in a shared space, or if a friend of your Partner knew about your behaviors, this information will be important for your Partner to know. These places, people, and acting-out environments will be important for your Partner to know in order to help with the grieving process as well as to make choices about whether to keep them in her daily life. Similarly, those people will also be impacted in the future. For example, if a friend or family member of your Partner knew about your acting-out behaviors or colluded with you, your Partner may need boundaries around your interacting with them in order to rebuild a sense of safety moving forward.

Discloser Misconception 6: This is too painful for my Partner – She is only doing this for "pain shopping"

This notion that Partners are seeking a FD as a way of pain shopping is antiquated. We now see a FD as an important step in rebuilding safety and trust in a relationship. Of course, the FD will be painful. Yet as we have already discussed, the pain of NOT doing a FD can be excruciating for Partners. Additionally, whether it be a broken bone or a broken heart, healing involves pain. Healing without pain is an unrealistic expectation. The task for disclosure is not to avoid the pain but to prepare in a way that the pain is the type that comes with healing.

Discloser Misconception 7: Doing a disclosure and adding a polygraph is all about shaming me

It can be daunting for you to think about disclosing your sexual secrets. It makes sense that you could feel shame for your behaviors mixed with fear for having the behaviors be exposed to the person you care most about.

That said, a Full Disclosure is NOT about shaming. It is not an inquisition or a trial. The goal is to have you share your sexual behaviors to build a new foundation in your relationship based upon truth. In our experience, this process is deeply honoring and can be a sacred experience for couples. As disclosure guides, we work to make sure that the Rite of Truth is a safe place for all.

You may feel shame in this process, but feeling shame is not the same thing as being shamed. As you will no doubt be learning in your recovery outside of this disclosure journey, the goal is for you to separate shame from guilt. Guilt focuses on your actions; shame focuses on who you are. The FD is about your behaviors, not about who you are as a person. One simple way we can differentiate guilt from shame is to say, "I have done bad things" (guilt) vs. "I am bad" (shame). Your disclosure guide will work to not have this be a shaming environment, while at the same time allowing you the space to take full responsibility for your actions and to feel the emotions that result.

Discloser Misconception 8: My Partner is going to use this information in divorce proceedings

The goal of a disclosure is NOT to use the information in divorce proceedings. While we can't predict if couples will or will not stay together after the FD, the purpose of going through this process with your Partner is to give a foundation of truth in order to rebuild intimacy in your relationship. The goal is not to go through a disclosure in order to gain more information for a divorce or separation.

For this reason, if you or your Partner are actively seeking to leave the relationship, we would strongly advise you to talk with a trained professional before you go through this workbook and through a FD. We HAVE seen situations where completing a Full Disclosure process can be invaluable for Partners and Disclosers alike, even in situations where divorce or permanent separation is present. These situations are delicate and multifaceted. Please consult with your disclosure guide and legal counsel before forging ahead with this workbook if you are considering divorce.

Fear that your Partner will leave is understandable, even if no action toward divorce has been taken. And while we can't predict what will happen in your particular situation, according to Schneider, Corley, and Irons in a survey of 164 recovering addicts and their Partners, 60% of Partners threatened to leave after the initial confession, but 72.4% of them did not follow through with separating. And in the same study, nearly 42% of the respondents reported holding back information from their Partners.[7] One has to wonder if the continued withholding contributed to leaving the relationship for those who did follow-through on their threats. So again, talk to your disclosure guide about your concerns to ensure safety for your disclosure process. And if you do decide to move forward with disclosure, tell the truth!

Discloser Misconception 9: Doing this Full Disclosure is futile: It is never going to be enough for my Partner... I'll do this and she'll just want something more right after.

It is common for the disclosing party to have negative core beliefs about not being "enough" for others, and especially toward their Partner after sexual betrayal. We have frequently heard variations of this sentence from individuals prior to disclosure.

You may be early in the healing journey after discovery or initial disclosure. You may be trying everything and it still doesn't seem to be enough to help your Partner heal. You may be feeling hopeless, frustrated, dejected, angry, demoralized, or some other feeling as a result. We get it, and we'll be offering words of encouragement from others who have gone through this journey before you.

That said, your Partner is going through an incredibly painful journey right now, perhaps the most intense pain ever experienced. Unfortunately, this pain was initiated by your actions. It WILL take time for your Partner to heal, and there isn't one thing, even disclosure, that will make the pain go away. Understand that your Partner WILL have needs from you post disclosure.

Remember your purpose in disclosure: It is not to have your Partner "get over it" and "move on" - we have already addressed that stance; it doesn't work. Your purpose is to provide a new foundation of truth as you do the Full Disclosure. And your healing journey from sexual betrayal doesn't END post disclosure. It would be like saying a house was completed because you poured a solid concrete foundation. This disclosure, done well, will provide a new solid foundation for your relationship to heal. So, disclosure is where your relationship healing can START.

Discloser Misconception 10: If my Partner is angry, hurt, sad, scared or distrustful during or after the disclosure that means I shouldn't have disclosed.

This misconception goes along with some others that we have already discussed. As you will see in the disclosure benefits and risks exercise to come, it is likely that your Partner will be angry after disclosure. This is normal. Take a moment and reflect. Put yourself in her shoes. If the roles were reversed and your Partner were sharing the betrayals that you're about to share with her, how would you feel? Would you be happy and relieved? Or would you be hurt? Betrayed? Angry? Would you then feel ready to go right back to the relationship as you knew it? We imagine you would likewise have strong feelings if the roles were reversed.

We recognize that anger can be scary, especially after you have shared such devastating information. Just remember that this is part of your Partner's healing journey. As you hold space for your Partner's feelings, her anger will begin to transition into hurt, pain, rejection, and sadness. This is a gift of vulnerability that your Partner will give you, a gift that she will need to feel safe enough to give you. You can have a huge role in allowing this vulnerability to flourish, but it does start with anger, and frequently anger after FD.

If your Partner has taken full responsibility for coping with the level of detail that she has requested from you (and this workbook will help her take that responsibility), then your job is not to regret that you told her. It is to regret that you did those things that hurt her. Coming to accept this will be part of your recovery work going forward. Your Partner needs to feel emotions; it is part of her grief. Neither she nor your relationship will be able to move forward until she goes through it. Your behavior going forward will tell her how willing you are to support her through her grief process.

We do understand that it can be difficult to be present with your Partner's intense emotions. To help with this, we will be providing tools for both of you to better prepare for the process. Just know that intense emotions during and after the Rite of Truth are normal.

References:

[4]*Magness, M. (2009).* Hope & Freedom for Sexual Addicts and Their Partners. *Cave Creek, AZ: Gentle Path Press.*

[5]*Jill Manning, e-mail message to author, March 12, 2019.*

[6]*Association of Partners of Sex Addicts Trauma Specialists. (2019). APSATS Multidimensional Partner Trauma Model Training: Module 3: Discovery Trauma and Crisis and Module and Module 4: Disclosure Trauma. Cincinnati, OH: Independently Published.*

[7]*Schneider, J.P, Corley, D.M., and Irons, R.R. (1998). Surviving Disclosure of Infidelity: Results of an International Survey of 164 Recovering Sex Addicts and Partners. Journal of Sex Addiction & Compulsivity 5(3), 189-218.*

SECTION THREE:
HEALING FROM OUR OWN PERSONAL EARTHQUAKE

OUR PERSONAL RELATIONSHIP DISASTER

We have spent some time exploring disclosures, what they are and what are not, as well as some common misconceptions about disclosure. Now let's take a few moments to explore where a disclosure may fit in your healing journey. To do this, it is helpful to use a metaphor of recovery after a disaster as a way to look at this process.

Disasters, both natural and human-made, are catastrophic. They affect our health, safety, relationships, well-being, families, careers, and our environment. Healing after a catastrophic event takes time and intention. It may require the assistance of outside professionals or services. Recovery takes dedicated time and focused energy. Human-made disasters, especially those that involve betrayal, can be even more difficult to recover from.

Disasters have predictable phases: Response, Recovery, and Maintenance. These phases look something like this:

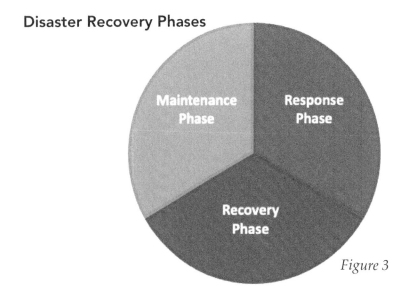

Figure 3

First after a disaster comes the **Response Phase.** In this phase, emergency teams are sent to secure the safety of affected structures, to protect and tend to anyone affected, and to prevent anyone else from being harmed by the disaster. It is vital for rescue teams to move swiftly to minimize the negative effects of the disaster.

Similarly, in your situation, you just got hit by a detrimental, spouse-generated earthquake after discovery of sexual betrayal. In this time of crisis, you have most likely sought safety, as well as a way of immediately understanding the damage done. Your rescue team may take the shape of a therapist, a coach, a clergy member, a safe recovery website, a support group, or this workbook. This is the time to establish **SAFETY, SAFETY, SAFETY.** Building a support network of safe individuals as well as new skills to help you ground yourself in new ways will help protect you and minimize the impact of this rupture in your life. We'll have resources in Volumes Two and Three of the this workbook series that are designed to help you build safety in response to the betrayal-earthquake that has shaken you.

The second phase after a disaster is the Recovery Phase. By this point, rescue teams have saved all those who are able to be saved, the wounds of those affected have been tended to, and structures have been secured for basic safety or cleared if they have been deemed unsafe. In the Recovery Phase, an in-depth assessment is carried out to determine the full extent of the damage of the disaster. Based on this assessment, a course of treatment is created and carried out. Obviously, this phase can be quite extensive and costly. Recovery may take some time to fully carry out as well.

For you, post discovery, the **Recovery Phase** will similarly take some time. This phase involves a fuller understanding of the impact of sexual betrayal on you and on your relationship. It is also a time for grieving all the losses of the life you had, or thought you had, including the structure of your previous relationship. That structure crumbled when your personal earthquake hit and sexual betrayal was discovered. This recovery process will require support, patience, and pain, but it will also bring you to a new self and hopefully a new relationship, stronger than before.

Finally, in the **Maintenance Phase,** all the work of the Response and Recovery phase is maintained in the future. This entails incredibly important work to prevent excess damage from future disasters and, in some cases, to prevent the disaster itself. We need to remember that maintenance does NOT mean losing focus. Quite the opposite! The maintenance phase requires active daily work to ensure the safety of structures, and to make sure that no further disasters occur in the future.

For you, in the aftermath of sexual betrayal, this means to continue to do your own individual healing work, as well as further relationship intimacy work on a consistent basis as you go forward. This will solidify you and your relationship, lessening the possibility of future earthquakes from wreaking havoc on your relationship.

We hope this disaster metaphor helps you to better understand the healing journey for you and your relationship. Just as the course of action after an earthquake differs based on which phase you may be in, we have also found that what type of disclosure you may need will also depend on which phase of healing you are in after the earthquake. To look at the different types of disclosures available, let's put them on a continuum.

DISCLOSURE ON THE CONTINUUM

A crucial point to remember in preparing for your FD is that one size does not fit all. The type of disclosure you need will vary based on your phase in the healing process and your unique needs. Our intent here is to educate you about the differences you will likely experience in reviewing the literature, questioning different guides, and discussing FD with recovery peers. It can be confusing when you receive different information from different people. Sometimes the confusion is created because they are all actually describing different FDs.

Disclosures occur on a continuum and there is no one universally agreed-upon standard for going about them. The right fit for one couple may be wrong for another. Disclosures on the continuum are characterized by such factors as the nature and format of the information shared, resources and community support used in the process, the methods used in the FD process, and the amount of time spent in recovery before completing the FD.

Denial and Truth

Denial is an issue that complicates recovery and can be a wild card in the disclosure process. In this sense, denial is not just a lie told to cover up betrayal; it is a psychological defense mechanism used to protect oneself from accepting a painful truth. Denial can include your spouse's refusal to admit the truth (aka lying), as well as different levels of psychological compartmentalization, from missing minor details to filing away major facts out of sight and out of mind. Denial can occur anywhere on the continuum, but it is almost always a major barrier in disclosures that occur earlier in recovery.

Recovery Phase and Truth

Other notable features that can distinguish between types of FD include the setting it takes place in, the coordination of the professionals involved, and the protocols of the professionals guiding your FD. At each point along the continuum the risks, benefits, and impact on subsequent recovery differ. Understanding where the FD you are preparing for is at on the continuum will help you develop more realistic expectations of the outcome.

For example, a disclosure during the Response Phase (see figure 3, earlier in this volume) would occur shortly after discovery when you are still in shock and your spouse has had little time in recovery or little sustained sobriety. Disclosures at this phase rarely result in a full and complete story. Personal recovery requires us to be a little bit like an archeologist, sifting through the dirt and digging up bits and pieces of our own history. When we put those dug up pieces together, they tell our personal story. Yet this archeological dig may require time and dedicated focus.

If your spouse is in early in recovery, he may not be motivated to put the necessary work into the dig because the pieces tell an ugly story that he may not want to face. Consequently, the betrayal story may be sketchy and be based on an "only as much as I have to" energy. Alternatively, he may throw himself into the task of finishing this process quickly in the false belief that digging fast is the same as digging thoroughly and will lead to a fast recovery. You might be tempted to believe that, too. Early on, he - and you - may be tempted to think he has exhumed all the pieces with relatively little time and effort. However, digging deeper almost always results in discovering additional fragments that change the pattern of the story.

Discovery and Shock Trauma

Similarly, Partners often go in and out of shock for a significant period of time after the discovery of their spouse's secret life. Shock trauma has a major impact on one's emotional life, physical functioning, and concentration abilities. Consequently, due to the overwhelming impact of discovery, you may feel pressured to make major life decisions at the time that you are still reeling from aftershocks. This can set up an expectation that a disclosure earlier in the recovery process can somehow end the pain or prevent the need to do the deeper healing work.

If you and your spouse are aware of these pitfalls with an early recovery FD, you are less likely to be demoralized when previously compartmentalized omissions and distortions come to light, or additional pieces of excavated truth are uncovered. If this is the case, you can build in a "how do we handle it if" boundary as part of your post-Truth Rite coping plan process. Then, when additional pieces are unearthed, you can have your feelings about it and stick to the plan, even if it means that down the road an additional FD is necessary. In Volume Two, we will provide you a boundary guide post-disclosure to help you and your spouse better navigate your coping plan after your Rite of Truth.

Disclosure and Wait Time

While there are pitfalls with an early FD, there are also risks if couples wait too long to do disclosure. Waiting too long to do a FD is like building a new structure after an earthquake without having secured the foundation. The trust and safety you have built may come crashing back down when new information comes to light. Additionally, healing may be stalled for couples who wait too long to do disclosure, which can have huge negative impacts on intimacy.

It is important for us to talk about the different types of disclosure, and the factors that may lead to each type of disclosure, to better help you prepare for where you are on the continuum, what you can expect, and how you can move through this process in the best way possible.

Disclosure Continuum

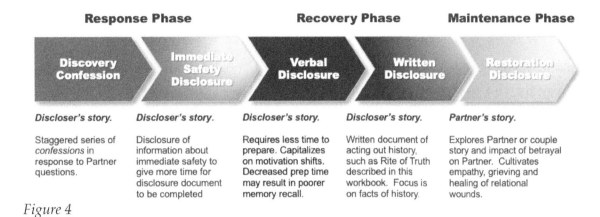

Figure 4

Graphically, we can break down the disclosure continuum like this:

As you can see from this chart, you'll notice the three main phases of the FD process we addressed above: Response Phase, Recovery Phase, and Maintenance Phase. Disclosures done during each of these three phases will all look different. Just as we mentioned previously about the three phases of recovery from a disaster, you can see that the path of healing from sexual betrayal follows a similar course.

When an earthquake decimates a town, responders need to know the extent of the damage before they can take action for repair. First responders must evaluate structural integrity of buildings to determine how safe it is for those trying to help to enter buildings, clear debris, or search for survivors. Ultimately, they assess initial safety, add temporary supports that prevent further collapse while they detail the extent of the damage, and finally, work toward recovering from the damage done. In the same way, you can see these three phases of healing in your own personal disaster depicted in Figure 4.

Disclosures in the Response Phase

In the direct aftermath of a disaster, we need to determine the extent of the damage. And in cases of sexual betrayal, a series of staggered disclosures and **discovery confessions** often follow immediately after discovery of the betrayal. Though we recognize these confessions do happen frequently, we do not consider them to be professionally-led and are certainly not therapeutic. These generally occur as a series of confessions generated by Partner questions, by the Partner finding evidence, if the Discloser thinks he is about to be caught, or by him sharing secrets to alleviate his own guilt. We have found that often these confessions involve partial truths, minimizations, justifications, or other withheld information that will ultimately become more damaging when those details are discovered or disclosed down the road. If you are in this Response Phase, we encourage you to consult with your disclosure guide and use this book to support your disclosure process immediately.

That said, if you have foundational needs for safety right now, an **immediate safety disclosure** is a way for you to receive vital information before your spouse is ready to give his Full Disclosure to you. This type of disclosure is typically a verbal response to well-chosen questions. They are sometimes driven by a polygraph to help answer a few fundamental questions about issues requiring an immediate response, such as whether children are safe in the Discloser's presence or are being exposed to sexual behavior, if deception is jeopardizing your financial security, legal action is imminent, the betrayals are about to be exposed to the public, or if you may have been exposed to sexually-transmitted infections. This type of disclosure gives you the benefit of receiving important safety information in a relatively quick amount of time. However, one major drawback of an immediate safety disclosure is that these types of disclosures are not typically complete disclosures. For that reason, you may need to wait weeks or even months before receiving the completed FD. In addition, because these disclosures occur relatively quickly, they may not give you adequate time to put a good coping plan together. It can be rather like jumping before ensuring the safety net has been secured.

If you believe you need an immediate safety disclosure right now, please see Appendix 1 for more information on what these types of disclosures can look like.

Disclosures in the Recovery Phase

After the Response Phase comes the **Recovery Phase** of healing. As with any kind of assessment, attending to details gives a clearer picture of what the pattern of carnage is. Just as it is difficult to itemize a full and complete inventory of personal items lost immediately after a disaster, it is difficult to get a full inventory of betrayals in the Response Phase. FDs that occur later in recovery, after your spouse has had some sustained sobriety and has spent time digging thoroughly into his own history, are less likely to involve significant omissions and distortions due to memory-related issues.

However, every choice has a consequence, and with a deeper dig comes a longer time before the FD can occur. For some couples, you may find that the greater quality is worth the wait; for others, maintaining secrets fuels shame such that the deeper dig can't start until AFTER the secrets are revealed. For still others, the wait time can become prolonged and create additional pain in the relationship so that the fragments he is digging through keep piling higher and higher and they are most likely being piled on top of you. The bulk of the preparation you will do through this workbook serves as a resource for you during this Recovery Phase of your healing journey. We will be focusing on a **written disclosure** in this workbook, but we did want to first state that there are other types of disclosure processes for you to consider that do not involve a written disclosure document.

Verbal disclosures are detailed accounts of sexual betrayal and are often done more quickly than a formal disclosure with a written document. They may be done in an intensive setting facilitated by a therapist, or perhaps after you have gotten into initial recovery. There are benefits and drawbacks of a verbal as opposed to a written disclosure. Verbal disclosures require less preparation, so they can often be facilitated earlier in the process. Since they require less preparation and set up, they can capitalize on moments when your spouse's motivation to disclose is high, before that moment passes. They may sometimes be accompanied by a fidelity polygraph that increases motivation for an honest accounting of transgressions and can help provide a level footing for you in the relationship. Verbal disclosures are best done with a guide who is experienced at conducting these types of disclosures. Because there is less structure involved in a verbal disclosure, the experience of the disclosure guide is more critical to achieving a quality outcome.

However, a significant drawback of verbal disclosures is that they are generally done earlier in the Recovery Phase of the process. Consequently, the Discloser will often not have done adequate work to understand the full impact of his behaviors on both you and your relationship and will still have more work to do to break through compartmentalized memories. As a result, more repressed information may surface later, and he may be more likely to react defensively or spiral into shame during a verbal disclosure process than if he had more time to focus on dealing with emotional reactivity that comes up when writing the disclosure document. The time spent working and reworking a written disclosure document offers more opportunity to target and alter underlying patterns of shame and distorted thinking that serve as barriers to empathy and understanding.

As we stated above, this workbook will focus on a **Written Disclosure** process. A written disclosure is a structured process where your spouse prepares a document that includes a history of his sexual behaviors. It often also includes answers to specific questions that have been posed by you and is structured according to the level of information you are needing. Although lying by omission or commission, cognitive distortions, defensiveness, shame, and lack of empathy can and do occur in written disclosures, the process of developing the document and working through multiple edits and revisions with a skilled and experienced disclosure guide often deepens the process of breaking through his denial. This is one major benefit of a written disclosure: A more complete transfer of truth in the Rite of Truth. The writing of the document affords him the opportunity to identify and develop a plan to cope with the emotions that will arise while he is disclosing.

One drawback of a written disclosure is time: as you can see in the pages of this workbook, a written disclosure can take weeks and in some difficult cases, months to complete. That is one major reason we have written these companion workbooks: We believe that using them will help speed up the process for you and provide to you both a higher quality FD.

Because there are different disclosure types possible, it is important to carefully consider the options available to you. Make sure to talk with your disclosure guide about what type of disclosure is right for you and for your spouse.

Disclosures in the Maintenance Phase

The final phase of healing is the **Maintenance Phase.** In a disaster, this is where damage is repaired, restitution is made, and the new relationship foundation is carefully laid in a way that buffers you from the impact of future disasters. This is where restoration can occur. The main bulk of this healing will take place in the months and years after disclosure. Up to this point, in the Response Phase and Recovery Phase, FDs had emphasized the Discloser's story, where he put in varying levels of time and effort to dig through his past and put together the pieces of his betrayal history. In this later phase of healing, he now explores the impact his betrayal had on you. At the same time, you put the information about his betrayal history together and use it to reconstruct and understand your own history - what was going on in your life when the betrayals occurred, how they impacted you, and how you can empower yourself in the future. This is your greater truth; this is YOUR story. Now the story of your relationship - the story of "We" - and the intimacy pyramid can transform with a new, richer meaning.

Maintenance Phase disclosures occur on a spectrum, from those that closely resemble the FDs that this workbook prepares you for, to those that follow after the initial FD. Disclosures in this category tend to occur much deeper in the recovery process, because to be effective, they require that some degree of tentative trust, an earned trust, has been established. This trust most likely occurs because there has been evidence that the emotional maturity of the Discloser, hence his capacity for empathy, has deepened as a result of his recovery efforts. Through that deepened trust, you may then be better able to allow yourself compassion for his story, without fear that it will be used as a tool of manipulation, that your pain will be dismissed, or that the your spouse will interpret your compassion as "mission complete" with no further need to help you heal.

Maintenance Phase disclosures acknowledge that although you have a story too, it is rarely given equal status to your spouse's in disclosures associated with the earlier phases.

Maintenance Phase disclosures signal the transition from his story to your story, from you investing time and emotional energy in understanding his story to him becoming as interested in learning your story as you were his. Notice that this requires more than him being able to adequately reflect your pain or understand a piece of your puzzle in a given moment, with no retention or interest in how that piece fits together in the puzzle of your story. Instead, it requires that he becomes increasingly invested in how his choices altered your story and who you are becoming in recovery.

Maintenance Phase disclosures are disclosures that can come after a FD, or after you are already aware of much of your spouse's history of betrayals. Alternatively, a disclosure may be combined with additional rituals aimed at relationship repair. In this instance, the main focus isn't just on truth as a foundation, but truth as well as the other elements of the intimacy pyramid, including intimacy. We call these types of disclosures **Restoration Disclosures.** Different guides have different methods for facilitating these types of disclosures. Consequently, a Restoration Disclosure can be a part of a combined FD and rituals of repair and restoration, or it can follow sometime after the FD as a stand-alone ceremony symbolizing transition to empathy as a healing ritual.

One example of this type of disclosure is a **validating disclosure**, developed by recovery and relationship expert Doug Weiss.[8] A validating disclosure doesn't fit neatly into a specific location on the continuum because it is both an honoring of your story and a tool for encouraging the betrayer's continued empathy development. As such, it can occur earlier than the Maintenance Phase as an exercise to spur your spouse to attune to the impact of betrayal on you and to begin the process of empathy for that impact. It can also occur much later in the Maintenance Phase as a ceremony, consolidating the development of mutual empathy that has already occurred.

In a validating disclosure, your spouse shares more than just his sexual behaviors. He now acknowledges these behaviors and their impact during key times in your life. A validating disclosure moves from a focus on his story of sexual betrayal to your story of betrayal impact. The energy shifts from both of you seeking to understand his story to both now seeking to understand *your* story. Restoration Disclosures, such as this form of a validating disclosure, symbolize that shift, as well as the transition to begin creating a new understanding, a new meaning, and a new story for your relationship – a new story of We. Such a disclosure provides a new foundation for shared intimacy birthed from grieving the loss of the previous relationship, followed by the unified experience of rebuilding a new one. Validating disclosures represent one form of a Restoration Disclosure. We will be describing Restoration Disclosures more in future resources, but we encourage you to talk to your disclosure guide about any guidelines they have for such a disclosure. Whatever the format, a Restoration Disclosure can be a powerful process for a couple, as it builds a new level of intimacy based on shared pain and grief.

Many Partners understandably are seeking a FD that includes all the elements described in these Maintenance Phase disclosures, that is, a combined FD as we are presenting in this workbook, as well as a Restoration Disclosure – these disclosures aim at moving beyond a new foundation based on truth to honoring a new level of intimacy. We are aware of experienced guides who only sanction FDs of this nature. Yet we also recognize that, depending where you are in the recovery journey, emotional maturity and empathy may take months or, in some cases, years, to properly engage. For many Partners, the extended period of time of not knowing the exact nature of the betrayals, takes too great a toll and adds additional deep cracks in the relationship foundation. We have heard from many couples who in early recovery didn't fully comprehend how long it could take to be able to participate in this type of FD and, consequently, came to feel frustrated and blocked by guides who only advocate for Maintenance Phase FDs. FDs that don't metaphorically hit it out of the park risk the potential gains not being worth the wait. We are aware of many Partners who waited until the Maintenance Phase for any form of disclosure because they falsely believed they knew most of the betrayals already. In these cases, the pyramid has been rebuilt on shaky ground and shattered again when major deceptions were revealed: the validation and empathy they had anticipated being honored came to represent a recovery con.

For that reason, the focus of this workbook will be on a Written Disclosure during the Recovery Phase of healing. We believe that this type of disclosure strikes a helpful balance between a FD of betrayals earlier in the process, while still moving toward a separate **Restoration Disclosure** as the healing of your relationship foundation solidifies.

Summary

After participating in many disclosures at different points along the continuum, using different formats along the way, we have developed a professionally-guided FD preparation process that we have found to honor the recovery for you, your spouse, and your relationship, and we would like to share it with you. This workbook series will focus on a written disclosure format, helping you prepare to receive the information shared as well as how to best navigate the process.

Now that we have looked at how disclosures occur on a continuum, let's take a moment to determine where you and your spouse fall on this continuum to see if a disclosure is right for you. Afterward we will review some steps you can take to select a good disclosure guide and talk about what the Rite of Truth generally looks like.

References:

[8] *Weiss, D. (2007). Validating Disclosure: AASAT Training Course. American Association for Sex Addiction Therapy. Anaheim, CA: Discovery Press.*

SECTION FOUR:
WHAT DOES THIS LOOK LIKE FOR US?

SHOULD WE DO A DISCLOSURE?

We have talked about the overall healing journey for couples impacted by sexual betrayal as well as how a FD fits into this healing process. We have explored some common misconceptions about the disclosure process and shared some different types of disclosure. Before you move to preparing for your Rite of Truth, it is important to take a look at some potential pros and cons of going through this process so you can make an informed decision about participating in it. This will help you get a realistic picture of what you might expect from the process, so your expectations can better match what you'll be receiving in the FD. Ultimately, knowing the benefits and risks of a FD will help make the experience as safe and successful as it can possibly be.

For the following exercise, place a check mark beside any of the potential benefits, as well as any potential risks, that resonate with your particular experience about engaging in a disclosure. We have provided a few additional spaces for you to add which apply to specifically to your situation.

Disclosure Benefits and Risks for you as a COUPLE:

Benefits:

☐ Helps your coupleship find and/or re-establish a new story of We

☐ Helps create a foundation to begin rebuilding from betrayal by putting all secrets out on the table

☐ Puts both of you on an equal playing field of information

☐ Builds a foundation to develop earned trust based on truth

☐ Establishes a new burgeoning intimacy based on vulnerability

☐ Helps you find a footing for a secure base in the future

☐ Cleans out the infected "wound" that lies created, helping give your relationship the best opportunity to heal

☐ Interrupts repeated power struggles over the history of betrayals

☐ Other potential benefit for your coupleship: _____

_____

_____

☐ Other potential benefit for your coupleship: _____

_____

_____

Risks:

- ☐ Just as in a surgery, things often get worse before they get better; in the short-term it may seem like the relationship has gotten "worse" for a while as you grieve the losses
- ☐ It is possible that a FD may be too much for your relationship to bear – you may separate or your relationship may end as a result (however, it is usually the CONTINUED betrayals and lies, not the FD, that will kill a relationship)
- ☐ It may lead to consequences: legal, interpersonal, work, family, etc.
- ☐ Depending on what the truth is, a FD may impact relationships with friends, family, co-workers
- ☐ It may limit certain places, experiences, activities etc. that you will engage in in the future, depending on specifics of shared information (who, what, when, where, how). If illegal sexual activity or abuse is disclosed, a report to relevant authorities may be required based on the laws governing the location where you are doing your FD
- ☐ Disclosures can be painful, sometimes traumatic, even when done well

- ☐ Other potential risk for your coupleship: _____

_____

_____

- ☐ Other potential risk for your coupleship: _____

_____

_____

Disclosure Benefits and Risks for YOU:

Benefits:

- ☐ Gives you TRUTH: brings you out of the darkness of "not knowing" and into the light of the facts

- ☐ Helps you understand your spouse's past and the escalation of his behaviors

- ☐ Understanding his history of betrayal helps you create your own story, now based on truth. Your story to this point has been based on partial truths. After the FD, you will be able to rebuild a new story in life based upon all that was occurring in your relationship. This will help validate your intuition and your sense of what is real in your relationship

- ☐ Helps calm your nervous system and is a starting point for healing
- ☐ Helps you to grieve the losses, so that you can start to rebuild yourself and your relationship
- ☐ Helps you to make more informed choices about your relationship, your family, and your own healing
- ☐ Other potential risk for you: _____

_____

_____

- ☐ Other potential risk for you: _____

_____

_____

Risks:

- ☐ Can exacerbate betrayal trauma symptoms, particularly if you are not adequately prepared
- ☐ Can impact your relationships with friends, family, etc.
- ☐ Can be painful for you to hear and to make sense of what you learn
- ☐ Can take time to process
- ☐ May lead to separation
- ☐ May decrease trust in your spouse, depending on what you learn and whether he conducts himself with maturity and integrity
- ☐ Other potential risks for you: _____

_____

_____

- ☐ Other potential risks for you: _____

_____

_____

Disclosure Benefits and Risks for Your SPOUSE:

Benefits:

☐ Helps your spouse better understand your experience, helping him to build empathy as he sees the impact of his behaviors on you and others

☐ Helps him see the full extent of his behaviors, their potential escalation and unmanageability over time, as well as to see patterns in his behaviors he may have overlooked in prior recovery work

☐ Helps him relieve shame by no longer keeping secrets. By disabling and sharing his secret life, this process can help him let go of shame

☐ Honors himself and you by stepping up to the plate to admit the truth

☐ Serves as a living amends to you for the behaviors he has done

☐ Helps you see that he is doing "whatever it takes" to heal his relationship

☐ Builds a new foundation of truth, honesty, and integrity for himself and for your relationship

☐ Other potential risks for him: _____

_____

_____

☐ Other potential risks for him: _____

_____

_____

Risks:

☐ His relationship with you may get worse and may not even survive

☐ He will need to challenge core beliefs/fears which will feel uncomfortable. For example, "If she knew everything, she'd abandon me"

☐ Can damage relationships at work, with friends, family, etc.

☐ In the short-term, things will most likely be more difficult and his relationship with you may feel shakier

☐ Your preoccupation, questions, and distress may increase temporarily and he will feel the discomfort of facing your pain, grief, anger, or other difficult feelings and experiences

☐ Other potential risks for him:_____

_____

_____

☐ Other potential risks for him: _____

_____

_____

After completing this exercise on the benefits and risks of participating in a disclosure, I choose to:

☐ Move forward and complete a Full Disclosure
☐ Move forward without completing a Full Disclosure
☐ Move forward but will complete the Full Disclosure at some point in the future
☐ Unsure whether to move forward or not. Need more time to decide

Though we do believe that going through a Full Disclosure is beneficial, we recognize that going through this process is always your choice. Please make sure to talk to a trained professional about your choice above and what other options may exist for you to heal yourself and your relationship. It is important that you have carefully thought through the implications of your choice, making sure you are aware of all the pros and cons of your choice for your unique situation before you take action. An experienced guide can help you see blind spots in your analysis that you may have missed. Please make sure to get good support to help you heal from the damaging impact of betrayal in your relationship. Let's now look at some actual responses as to the benefits and risks of going through disclosure.

DISCLOSURE BENEFITS AND RISKS
(SURVEY RESPONSES)

Before moving on, we want to provide you results of our surveys for Partners and Disclosers on how their reported benefits and risks after having gone through a full disclosure and/or fidelity polygraph. We asked them the following questions, and here's what they had to say:

PARTNERS

Did you have fears about participating in a professionally-guided disclosure?

Seventy-seven percent of Partners reported they had fears about participating in the FD. As seen in Figure 5, of these, 51% reported that their fears were confirmed during the FD; 31% reported that some fears were confirmed and some were disconfirmed; while 10% indicated that their fears were disconfirmed.[8]

Partner Full Disclosure Fears

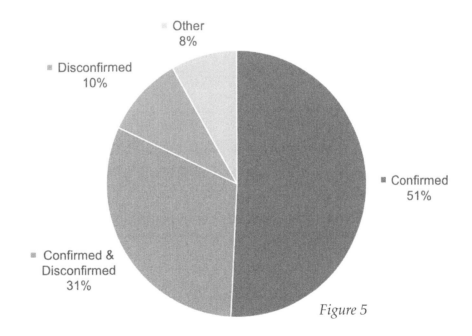

Figure 5

1. **FEAR OF LEARNING NEW INFORMATION**

   This was overwhelmingly the greatest fear for Partners.

   "Terrified. Completely terrified I would find out new information that I had not known. And I absolutely did."

   "Things would be worse than I had previously believed they were."

   "Fear of hearing truth I am not prepared in knowing. Fear that it is much worse than I realized."

   "That I was going to find out what he told me was the tip of the iceberg. It was."

   "That I would learn something that would make it impossible for me to stay in the relationship, or that might subject my husband to criminal charges."

   "Finding out things that I could not live with."

2. **FEAR THAT THE DISCLOSURE WOULD NOT BE TRUTHFUL AND COMPLETE**

   "I wouldn't get the truth."

   "That he would lie, minimize and blame and I would still not know the truth and have to wonder and doubt."

   "I was worried he was still lying."

   "Not get the truth. That the therapists would blame something on me and that they would minimize my spouse's actions and addiction."

3. **FEAR OF REACTIVATING OLD PAIN OF INFORMATION ALREADY KNOWN**

   "Bringing up old information and triggers."

Do you believe you were harmed as a result of participating in a professionally-guided disclosure?

NO = 50.9%

"I do not believe I was harmed. I believe it was completely necessary in me being able to move forward in my life and my marriage. As hard as it was, I believe it was priceless."

"Absolutely not. It's better to live in reality and I needed the truth to do so."

"I was protected. He was there with his counselor and I had mine. Very structured and safe."

"I have been harmed by him and his actions, both the sexually acting out and the lies. The disclosure, like all knowledge, is power."

"I was harmed in the same way you have to cut open an infected wound. It needed to be done, it would have been worse and festered and likely amputated if we hadn't cut it open. But it still hurt like heck."

YES = 36.8%

"No one had prepared me for the disclosure, I did not have a therapist, I was introduced to an advocate at the time of disclosure."

"Because his porn addiction was minimized."

"This was traumatic, I think I was so unprepared, I had no idea what he had done."

"I was not prepared by my therapist for the kind of trauma I would experience."

"I wasn't prepared for how bad it would be, the extent of his infidelity. I don't believe we had the most competent therapist to see it through."

"I was unprepared to hear it, my husband blamed me and I was not defended, he accused me and I was unable to defend myself. The disclosure took two separate sessions several days apart. The counselor showed no empathy for my pain. The counselor did nothing to coach me or guide me in asking questions so there were trickle disclosures over the next months...."

"There was little time given to process all the information or ask questions."

OTHER – YES AND NO = 12.3%

"It was the right thing to do but it does hurt knowing all the details."

"I was harmed by the betrayal that was confirmed in the information that was disclosed. Because I knew from discovery that there had been infidelity, I believe I would have been harmed more if we had not participated in a disclosure because of the answers my mind would have worked to create."

Do you believe you benefited as a result of participating in a professionally-guided disclosure?

YES = 86%

1. **DISCLOSURE HELPED UNDERSTAND BOTH DISCLOSER'S ADDICTION AND RECOVERY GROWTH**

    "It was an amazing opportunity to see my husband be honest and vulnerable all in the same place at the same time."

    "It got my husband honest; it made me face the extent of his addiction and how out of control it was. It let me know what it was I had to forgive and move past; I got to feel like he was treating me like an adult in this relationship. I got some power back – I got to see behind all the lies and decide for myself if I wanted to move forward in our relationship."

    "Has helped me to see the illness he has and the devastation to others he has done."

"I benefitted because finally someone else knew about my husband's behaviors and I heard some nasty things that put my husband's level of addiction in perspective."

"I know for sure this problem started in my husband's childhood. It didn't start in 2010 (which he had told me quite a while ago and attached blame to me)."

2. **EMPOWERED BY TRUTH**

"I am living truth for the 1st time in 44 years."

"I learned the truth. I deserve to know how I was betrayed."

"The disclosure helped me trust my gut and believe in my intuition. The times I was asking questions and was lied to or gaslighted were indeed times he was acting out. I did not enjoy listening to the disclosure, I literally scooted my chair back away from him as betrayal after betrayal came to my ears. But I needed to hear these things from his own mouth to continue the healing process."

"Feel like I know more than I would have without. More empowered by asking for and receiving the answer."

"Learning what exactly I was dealing with in terms of my husband's addiction. It helped me make an informed decision about whether or not I wanted to stay."

"I talk to many women who have yet to go through disclosure or whose husbands may not be in recovery and the fear that accompanies the unknown is worse. It causes people to not know what to fear, or how much to fear. Disclosure helped me confirm that I always knew that something wasn't right and it solidified that I will never let that 'feeling' being taken from me or manipulated away from me again."

"I got to put the pieces together – stuff started to make sense as far as timeline, behavior, etc."

"I knew where I stood in the relationship and more about the behaviors of the man I married. I was more in reality because of it."

"Some of the information disclosed validated what my intuition had told me over many years and I had been lied to about. It confirmed that I was not crazy and that I had been manipulated and lied to at every turn. Not a pleasant experience but it was part of my reality that had been denied for years and years."

"The guided disclosure included more viable information helpful to understanding what was really going on during a time of great confusion and hurt."

NO = 10.5%

1. DISCLOSURE WAS NOT FULL, TRUTHFUL AND BEHAVIOR DID NOT REFLECT TAKING FULL RESPONSIBILITY

"I did not benefit because the sexually acting out was minimized and I received a sanitized version that was not congruent or reflective of his sexual history timeline."

"The whole process was damaging. My needs were never considered, my timeline needs were completely disregarded. It was one more opportunity for him to abuse me, this time with his sex addicted therapist."

2. GUIDES MISMANAGED THE DISCLOSURE PROCESS

"The harms were mostly due to how my therapist handled it."

"I was not prepared by my therapist for the kind of trauma I would experience."

"I wish that I had never participated in this process with the former therapists."

"I unfortunately had 2 previous horribly-handled disclosures by a not-well-trained therapist. The third disclosure was done professionally and correctly."

"Therapist was not an expert on it. Allowed me to leave and go home alone afterwards and promoted staggered disclosure."

"I was unprepared to hear it, my husband blamed me and I was not defended, he accused me and I was unable to defend myself. The disclosure took two separate sessions several days apart. The counselor showed no empathy for my pain. The counselor did nothing to coach me or guide me in asking questions so there were trickle disclosures over the next months.... My husband was angry to even be there and made it clear he believed I'm what is wrong. The memory still stings because I'm not surprised at my husband's words but that the counselor could let him verbally kick me like that, repeatedly, and never step in."

"I was not seeing a therapist trained in sex addiction and betrayal trauma; she was a generalist and so she could not thoroughly prepare me. My ex was seeing a CSAT and he was aware of a local clinician who is APSATS trained, but I wasn't provided that information."

"My CSAT was great, his CSAT was not sensitive to Partner trauma.... It was like he was pouring salt in my wounds and I wasn't strong enough at the time to ask him to stop, though my CSAT did advocate for me by asking for a break."

"Here is my story and I appreciate the opportunity to share it. [My husband's] therapist was hostile, belittling and bullying toward me from the very beginning of the disclosure process. In retrospect, I feel highly traumatized by the experience and regret that I was put through it. As I was prepared by my therapist, I expected the disclosure to be pretty straightforward, [My husband] was to read his disclosure statement, I was to ask clarifying questions if needed and this would be our starting point for recovery. No touching, no apologies, just facts and clarity. I knew that it would be difficult to hear the disclosure information but after I did hear it, there was not much new information at that time. [My husband's] therapist had not met me previously but criticized me throughout. During disclosure I was told that I was partly to blame for [my husband's] behaviors, instructed that I will not ask... any more questions at any point, that I have problems with control since I am the spouse of a SA, my professional work is a sign of control, polygraph is another means of control, [my husband] is a victim of his upbringing ... These topics were brought up independently by the therapist. I was not prepared to handle this line of what felt like an attack. When I asked the 7-8 questions ... to clarify viewing in front of our children, money spent, accounts used, work computers used, etc., ... While the therapist belittled and bullied me repeatedly, [my husband] and my therapist remained completely silent. I have never felt less human or more isolated. A follow-up meeting was held that incorporated more of the same blaming and shaming behavior. Afterward, I felt like a complete basket case, sub-human and hopeless. I only have regrets about this experience."

YES and NO = 3.5%

"Emotionally, it was difficult. Ultimately, however, it gave me peace having it all come out and know I wasn't crazy."

Did the benefits outweigh the harms?

YES = 87.7%

1. **BENEFITS FOR THE PARTNER**

    "After getting past the frustration and disappointment, I feel stronger."

    "I would do it again. My therapist said to wait as it takes time while they sober up to even remember everything. My therapist was more confused that I was not overly angry. I felt relieved that I was not crazy, that he was doing what I thought he was doing."

    "I learned to trust my gut and that I will know what I need to know when I need to know it."

    "I had already made up my mind to heal with or without him. The disclosure helped me grasp the reality that my husband is not who I thought he was. It validated the red flags and gut feeling I had had for a long time that something was wrong. It encouraged me to seek a support group, counseling and support from trusted friends. It began the process of giving me a vocabulary to express what happened to me."

2. **UNDERSTANDING THE TRUTH AS A BENEFIT**

    "It harmed me, but a veil was lifted and I finally saw how dishonest he was capable of being."

    "The information in the disclosure gave me a starting place. Before disclosure I was spinning and spinning. I couldn't tell reality from lies, past from present and didn't know where to start."

    "While the disclosure was not complete and accurate, it gave me a good enough idea of his arousal template and insight into his acting out and repetitive trauma behaviors."

    "I finally knew the enormity of his addiction and betrayal."

"It allowed him to come clean. It allowed me to have knowledge of his behavior. He spent years making me feel like I was crazy, undesirable, etc. I now knew why. It doesn't make it any less traumatizing or excuse anything, but knowledge is power to heal."

3. BENEFITS FOR THE RELATIONSHIP

"The benefits were essential to moving forward as an individual and as a couple."

"We've repaired our marriage and are building a better one. This process gave me back my husband."

"In retrospect, yes, but I would have done it later and with someone who supported Partners more with more understanding of the Partner trauma model."

NO = 12.3%

"These are very difficult to not think about, especially the young traumatic episodes."

"Because I dissociated, I did not remember most of it."

I DON'T KNOW = 3.5%

References:

[9] The Hold on Sister Partner and Hang in There Buddy Disclosure Surveys are ongoing, online surveys tabulated by Caudill and Drake in 2018. These are informal surveys. As such, inferences about descriptive statistics should be interpreted with caution. Verbal responses are used with permission.

DISCLOSERS

Did you have fears about participating in a professionally-guided disclosure?

Ninety-six percent of the Disclosers reported they had fears about participating in the FD. The fears that the disclosing party shared revolved around a few main themes:

1. **FEAR OF THE RELATIONSHIP ENDING**

   "My wife filed for divorce 60 days after I admitted to my addiction. I was fearful the disclosure would be used against me to prevent me from seeing my sons. I was able to overcome the fear by realizing I could only control myself and not others and without disclosure I could never be the Dad I wanted to be."

   "Loss of relationship"

   "I was worried my wife would leave me."

   "Unrepairable damage from explicit content"

   "That the full truth of my transgressions would be the final nail in the coffin of my marriage. That I would fall apart during the disclosure or cause my spouse so much more pain that was unfair that I would lose it. That my spouse wouldn't acknowledge the facts as I gave them. That my spouse would take all of it and use it against me in any future issue."

   "Felt my Partner would never be able to forgive me for all that I had done."

2. **FEAR OF NEGATIVE IMPACT ON SELF**

   "Failure! Exposure-admitting my behavior to other persons. Coming face to face with the depth of my compulsive behavior. Shame. Truth."

   "That I would be thought of as more disgusting."

   "The shame of my actions. That I would not be believed."

"How embarrassed and shameful I'd feel with people knowing what I have done/thought."

"I had not told anyone about my behaviors before. I did not want to admit anything beyond what I had been caught at."

3. **FEAR OF PARTNER'S REACTIONS**
"Fear of retaliation. Divorce. Anger"

"Anger"

"The anger of my spouse"

"Fear of disclosing everything, fear of my wife's reaction, fear of actually saying what I wrote, fear of who I am - what type of monster am I to have done these things, fear of what will happen next"

4. **FEAR OF NEGATIVE IMPACT ON PARTNER**
"I was worried about the level of hurt for my wife."

"Wife's mental capacity to handle all the information."

"Worried about negative impact of the experience on my spouse."

5. **FEAR OF SOMETHING GOING WRONG WITH THE DISCLOSURE PROCESS**
"Will the poly work?"

"I was afraid of what I could not remember. Of the polygraph itself."

"I was worried I would fail my polygraph."

"False results from poly, vague questions leading to false negatives"

"That I was forgetting an acting-out partner, event, or detail"

"THE TRUTH"

Do you believe you were harmed as a result of participating in a professionally-guided disclosure?

NO = 66.7%

1. **DISCLOSURE BECAME ONE OF THE BEST EXPERIENCES OF MY LIFE**

   "All of the harm was self-inflicted as I replayed the destruction of 30 years of self-deception, lies, and my inside not matching the outside. The process of writing My Story and then writing my disclosure was a life changing process that brought many tears. 3 years post disclosure I can say it was my best moment after the birth of my 4 kids."

YES = 14.3%

1. **HARM BY THERAPIST'S RESPONSES**

   "My therapist acted in an unprofessional manner toward my spouse, making her the object of suspicion and brokenness."

2. **NEGATIVE IMPACTS ON SELF-ESTEEM AND SELF-WORTH**

   "My self-esteem and self-worthiness are crushed. It resurfaced feelings of being a sick and horrible person."

UNDECIDED = 19%

1. **DISCLOSURE HAD BOTH PROS AND CONS**

   "I believe there are pros and cons...BUT this was honoring my Partner's request."

   "Though I don't believe I was actually harmed, sometime it feels like having a bright light shone on that which had been hidden up to that moment was harmful - certainly at the time. It was not a pleasant experience."

2. **DISCLOSURE PROCESS WASN'T COMPLETED**

   "It is been more than 2 years since disclosure and my wife has not been given the chance to provide her impact statement. Now, the coaches seem to have her impact statement on the back burner, although she wanted to give it at the time of disclosure (a medical problem with a facilitator caused the process to be interrupted). The failure to complete the process has directly impacted our recovery in a bad way."

Do you believe you benefited as a result of participating in a professionally-guided disclosure?

YES = 90.5%

1. **DISCLOSURE HELPED BUILD TRUST**

   "Helped create some trust with my wife"

   "Rebuilding trust"

2. **DISCLOSURE GUIDES WERE HELPFUL**

   "Therapists were a huge help to make sure we both able to get [through] the disclosure [without] major issues"

   "The alternative is to do it piecemeal in a non-therapeutic environment that is not healthy for either party"

   "I wouldn't have wanted it any other way, it is nice to have neutral parties helping me work through emotions."

   "It was a safe environment for me to share with my wife and to get everything out in the open. While this was not the end of needing to disclose acting out to my wife, it did provide a clean slate (in a sense - no more lies/secrets)."

3. **DISCLOSURE CLEARED A NEW SPACE IN THE RELATIONSHIP OF HONESTY**

   "I was not harmed, I was liberated. Out from the weight of the shame, lies and betrayals I have been on a completely different trajectory as a result of the disclosure. My life, my self-respect, and my sense of worth have all improved dramatically."

   "All the secrets came out without as much pain as I thought."

   "I got everything out into the open and as a result, was able to work through healing from things that were previously hidden. If they had remained hidden, there is no way I would have gotten healing from them."

   "At this point there is relief from being fully known."

   "A huge burden of lies was lifted from me and I feel better about myself and more motivated to 'keep the slate clean'."

"Although I already started on my recovery it gives me cleaner slate. I got everything on the table."

"Allowed me to open and honest about my past."

"Finally, all the secrets were out."

"Got to find a new starting place to allow my relationship to either survive or go down on honest terms. Gave my Partner some clarity upon which to make rational decisions."

"I understand my pattern, my triggers but most important I am not afraid to ask for help."

"Cleared out the cobwebs of my memory... allowed me to become honest with myself for the first time in my life."

"It has allowed me to see the truth of who I am and the choices that I made and I can no longer hide that from myself. It gave my spouse at the time some confidence that she had a full understanding of my behavior."

"It is freeing to not have to carry the burden of the lies. The foundation of my marriage needs to be repaired if it is going to continue and I realize I love her and want to stay with her so this is an integral point. I need to be open so she can freely choose otherwise I'm keeping her still in the dark and not letting her in. The structure allowed for guidance for us both in managing the emotional stresses. There were a lot of pitfalls in the process I wouldn't have been able to manage on my own and would've ended in disaster for both of us."

NO = 4.8%

(This individual was the same person who reported their therapist had been unprofessional during disclosure)

MAYBE = 4.8%

"While there is benefit, and would recommend it to those in similar circumstances, for us, there is a substantial part of the process that is missing. My wife truly feels rejected by the professionals, on top of my betrayal. Not a good situation." (this is an individual whose disclosure process was never fully completed).

Did the benefits outweigh the harms?

YES = 81%

1. **BENEFITS FOR THE RELATIONSHIP**

   "There is no way healing would have happened if I had not disclosed."

   "Easier talking when nothing to hide."

   "Set a baseline for us to move forward with."

   "The fear of the unknown future was the most difficult part and now that it is completed and I'm onto the next part of the path faithfully it is easier. Taking my time through this allowed both of us to reset and now that I have been sober, I can be present and manage the truth."

2. **BENEFITS FOR SELF**

   "Yes, because it was in a more controlled environment and it afforded me the opportunity to deal with my past all at one time."

   "My wife did not want to participate in recovery (hers or couple) and there was a pending divorce filed. She wanted and deserved disclosure. I had never had to admit failure before that moment. Admitting and facing my failures and destruction allowed me to start to heal and find forgiveness for myself. And I am happy to say 3 years post disclosure I am finally at peace with me and I am still married. Most important, I am becoming the father to all 4 [children] that I have always wanted to be."

   "In active addiction I vacillated between feeling worthless and ashamed to God. The lies and betrayals weighed heavily upon my emotions and psyche. I was in a continuous loop of barely feeling alive to numbed out. I have benefited from self-compassion, self-respect, a sense of worth and vitality. My whole outlook on life has had a major perspective shift; no longer am I plodding along in life onto a fitting end to my surviving. Now, I have greeted each new day with enthusiasm and I am embracing the depth of intimacy and wide range of emotions as wonders of life's great experience. And not as the victim of circumstances beyond my desire or control."

   "My fears were not reality."

   "Getting the secrets out."

"Without disclosure, I'd remain stuck in my addiction."

"HONESTY allowed me to approach my 12-STEP program with a clear head."

"As difficult as [disclosure] was, I would choose it again in a heartbeat. Living hidden and alone is not living at all. For me, the polygraph was what forced me to let go of hiding for the first time. Being honest is still a daily choice, but it gave me a benchmark for the first time."

"I needed to confront and face the facts of my acting-out behaviors. Cataloging them and observing them from a neutral, non-judgmental standpoint helped me to begin to see the magnitude of my actions. Prior to disclosure, my minimization of these activities led me to believe I hadn't done "too" much."

NO = 4.8%

"My spouse is now highly agitated about being traumatized even more than what was revealed in disclosure."

UNDECIDED = 14.3%

"At this point it is hard to say because I don't know what the future will bring. If it helps save our marriage then, yes. I do believe it will help me in my recovery."

"I don't know how much longer we will go before completing the process, but each day the benefit is reduced and the harm increased" (this individual was never able to complete the disclosure process).

SUMMARY

A summary of the Partner and Discloser survey results is shown in Figures 6A, 6B and 6C. These charts display the results of the questions:

1. Do you believe you were harmed as a result of participating in a professionally-guided disclosure?
2. Do you believe you benefited as a result of participating in a professionally-guided disclosure?
3. Did the benefits outweigh the harms?

As you can see, despite the uncertainty and pitfalls involved, overall both the Disclosers and Partners considered the process beneficial.

Were you harmed?

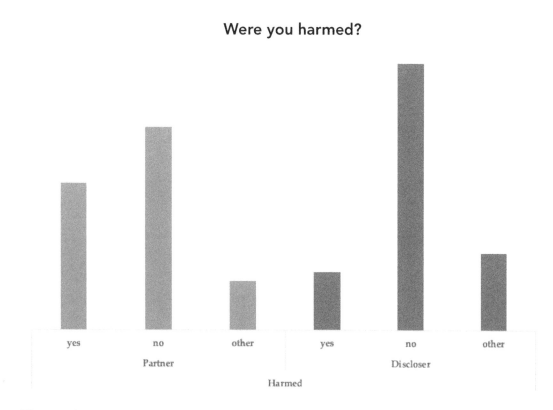

Figure 6A

Did you benefit?

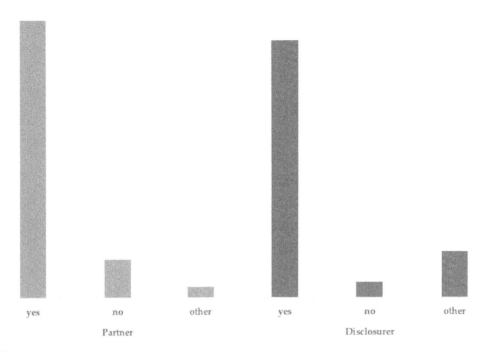

Figure 6B

Did benefits outweight harms?

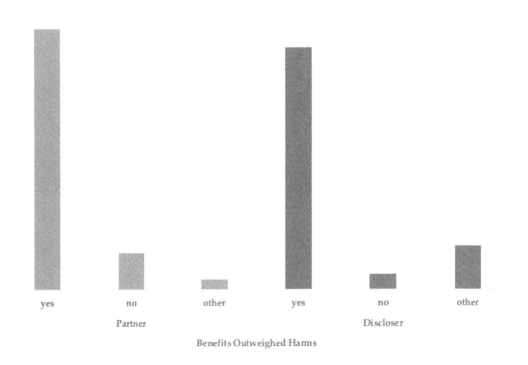

Figure 6C

Takeaways

What are the takeaways from these surveys? A) There are pros and cons associated with participating in this process. B) Despite the distress inherent in the process, the gains far outweighed the risks for the vast majority of people going through a FD. C) Many of the reported harms occurred as a result of poor preparation by disclosure guides, incomplete or poorly run disclosures, or other preventable issues by the guides. D) The right fit of the FD structure, the process of the disclosure, guide selection, and preparation are important factors in the outcome of a FD for both Partners and Disclosers.

The overall gains of FD are supported by two additional studies on disclosure – by Schneider, Corley, and Irons (1998)[10] and Carnes (2019)[11]. These studies concluded that greater than 93% believe that the FD was the right thing to have done. Let's now look at additional information from the research that Stefanie Carnes has conducted on healthy disclosures.

References:

[10]*Jennifer P. Schneider, M. Deborah Corley & Richard K. Irons (1998) Surviving disclosure of infidelity: Results of an international survey of 164 recovering sex addicts and Partners, Sexual Addiction & Compulsivity, 5:3, 189-217, DOI: 10.1080/10720169808400162*

[11]*Carnes, S. (2019). Executing an Effective Facilitated Disclosure. In Process.*

DISCLOSURE DONE RIGHT

Stefanie Carnes, PhD, completed research on the disclosure process. She identified 10 findings that surfaced out of her research about healthy, professionally-guided disclosures that we want to share here:[12]

- Healthy disclosures are generally for couples who are committed to one another.
- Healthy disclosures include adequate preparation for both parties.
- Healthy disclosures include appropriate levels of support.
- Healthy disclosures are very structured.
- Healthy disclosures contain only the appropriate level of information.
- Healthy disclosures allow you to have all the information you need clarified by allowing you to get all of your questions answered. If you do not want information then that is respected as well.
- Healthy disclosures are followed up by subsequent sessions to provide further clarity if necessary.
- Healthy disclosures are just the beginning of the healing process and you should be allowed to follow up with an impact statement.
- Healthy disclosures should be followed up with couples therapy and trauma treatment.
- While disclosure is very difficult, it is intended to be a healing process.

We have written the three volume workbook series as a way to accomplish all 10 of those findings in your Full Disclosure. Now that we've addressed the benefits and risks of going through with disclosure, and how to do it right, let's talk more about selecting a disclosure guide.

SELECTING YOUR DISCLOSURE GUIDE(S)

Once you have weighed the pros and cons about disclosure and decided to move forward with a Full Disclosure, it is important to find an experienced guide to help you through this process. If you are early in the healing journey, you may not have a team of support yet. You will be working on gathering your support team, and your disclosure guide will be an important part of this team. Similar to a quarterback in a football game, your guide will help you navigate this process in the most effective and successful way possible.

Disclosure guides come in many forms, but here are a few things you should consider when selecting a good disclosure guide:

1. **What is your prospective disclosure guide's experience with facilitating disclosures?**
   How much experience does your disclosure guide have in facilitating disclosures? Have they facilitated disclosures before? If so, how many? Just because someone is a licensed therapist, professional coach, faith leader, or are in personal recovery themselves doesn't necessarily mean they have experience preparing for and facilitating disclosures. Usually, understanding how to facilitate disclosures requires specialized training and experience. This leads us to the second issue to consider.

2. **What is your disclosure guide's training, both generally and SPECIFICALLY related to healing from Partner betrayal trauma and/or infidelity?**
   Having a doctoral degree in clinical psychology provides extensive training in working with individuals and/or couples across many different issues, but few degrees or training programs focus on the disclosure process; most don't even address it. Has your prospective disclosure guide received additional training, supervision, and/or experience in treating Partner betrayal trauma, infidelity, and/or sexual addiction? Therapists, coaches, and clergy can all receive additional training to better prepare them to facilitate effective disclosures. There are certifying organizations that provide specialized training in treating problematic compulsive sexual behaviors, sex/porn addiction and/or Partner betrayal trauma. These types of trainings typically address the FD process, although they may each emphasize different formats for working with disclosures on the continuum. We have included information about those organizations we are familiar with in Appendix 2. Feel free to ask prospective guides about additional training and certifications. Did the training or certification require a minimum amount of direct experience working with those who have experienced betrayal trauma, infidelity, or problematic sexual behavior or addiction before qualifying for the certification? If so, how much? Did the certification require supervision or consultation in order to receive the certification? The more direct,

supervised experience your guide has in this specialized field, the better prepared they will be to aid you in your disclosure.

Finally, make sure to inquire about how much experience your guide has in his or her respective profession in general. A professional may have training or a relevant certification but little professional experience to begin with. For example, depending on the training organization, a therapist can obtain a certification before being fully licensed. Similarly, a coach may have a certification but have only been actively coaching for a few months. In a disaster situation, do you want to be rescued by the EMS worker who just graduated or the seasoned veteran who has plenty of experience under the belt?

3. **Is the Partner guide training and experience comparable to the Discloser's guide and will you have ample time to develop a relationship with your guide prior to the disclosure?**
    Partners often initiate their counseling or coaching relationship through their spouse beginning his treatment; consequently, the referral for their own guide may be initiated by their spouse's guide. If this is the case, will you be working with someone with relatively little experience and little to no specific training in Partner betrayal trauma? If so, your recovery and FD preparation needs may not be seen as equal in status. Similarly, a misconception that professionals sometimes have is that completing a couple of sessions is adequate for preparing you for a FD. This may be the case if those sessions occur in an intensive or treatment center setting where the "session" may cover the course of several hours, the equivalent of weeks of outpatient therapy. In an outpatient setting, however, 2 sessions are inadequate preparation for facing a FD.

4. **Consider your location.**
    Not all locations have the same number of trained specialists in the area. For example, I (Janice), live outside the Dallas-Fort Worth metroplex and Dan lives in Los Angeles. Trained specialists are plentiful in heavily-populated areas such as these. There are a lot of qualified specialists in areas like these who do a wonderful job facilitating disclosures. However, there are many parts of this country and other parts of the world that do not have specialists. Although we advise against conducting the Rite of Truth from a distance when your guide is not physically present with you, if you're in a location where it is hard to find a qualified specialist you may consider working with a trained, certified distance therapist or coach who is not limited by geography. A distance guide can help lead you through the preparation process while you make other arrangements for the Rite itself. At other times, clergy members can receive additional training that make them a good option to consider as a guide. You can also use this workbook series to prepare you for an intensive option with facilitators experienced in the disclosure process.

5. **Determine your level of safety.**

   Part of the recovery journey involves leaning on others, as well as determining who is safe and who is not. As you interview a prospective disclosure guide, how do you feel with the person? Do you end the conversation feeling more emotionally safe or less safe? What do you notice in your body as you meet with her or him? How safe do you feel being completely transparent and vulnerable with this person? If he or she is a member of your community (e.g., in a clergy position), how safe will you feel after the FD, having shared all of this sensitive information? You want to make sure that the process is safe, and that your sensitive information is protected.

6. **What is your guide's philosophy of the process of healing from betrayal trauma?**

   It is always good to know what your guide's philosophy is in healing from betrayal trauma. How does s/he see this process? Is the impact of secretive sexual behavior on the relationship viewed as traumatic? What is the overall approach to couples healing? What is the philosophy or belief system about the process? What is the view on how much information is the right amount to share in a disclosure? It is important to know any biases that your prospective disclosure guide might have before you start the process. This also leads us to understanding your prospective guide's method to facilitating disclosures.

7. **What is your prospective disclosure guide's process for facilitating disclosures?**

   We have already shared that having specialized training and experience in doing disclosures is important. But now we want to see what your prospective disclosure guide's approach is. Can s/he walk you through a typical way that disclosures are conducted? Will the process be adapted to your unique needs or is it a one-size-fits-all procedure? Is the guide open to how you'd like this process to go? Does s/he advocate for a FULL disclosure? If not, how are decisions made about withholding information? What is the approach to working with other colleagues in the FD process? Collaboration is essential in having an effective disclosure, so you want to know how your guide will work with other colleagues. Can s/he describe to you how collaboration with other colleagues in disclosures occurs? Is there openness to working with the FD guides of your choice, or are you limited to only someone else in his or her practice?

   How long do clients generally wait before doing FDs? For example, does your spouse need to have a minimum amount of sobriety before a disclosure can occur? Are there stipulations on what will determine if your spouse is "ready" for the FD? How is it determined when you are "ready" to do a FD? Are there stipulations on determining if you are ready? If so, what are these stipulations, and how are unique situations that may arise handled (e.g., your spouse not able to maintain sobriety or the distress for you in WAITING for disclosure being greater than going through it?). Also, how difficult has it been for you to coordinate schedules with this professional? How difficult is it going to be for the guides to communicate with each other? Professionals who have busier schedules or limited flexibility may add more wait time to the disclosure process. Ask about how much time will be available on a weekly basis to help you prepare for your disclosure.

How do you feel about your prospective disclosure guide's methodology? How long does the professional generally take to prepare disclosures? How are both you and your spouse prepared for the disclosure? You want to make sure that both of you receive appropriate support along the way, and that this is carefully thought out and planned. We discourage the types of disclosures that are spontaneous and impulsive and occur in a single therapy session right after your spouse expresses a desire to do a disclosure. As you'll see in the pages to come, our belief is that effective written disclosures take some time to prepare.

Does the professional's process of FD fit for what you're wanting and needing? For example, will you have the opportunity to read the FD document during the Rite? Will the document be available to review with your guide for some time period after the Rite of Truth? Is the document available for your guide to review and give feedback on BEFORE the Rite? If so, is your guide willing to do this? Some Partner guides are uncomfortable knowing information that they cannot share with you before the Rite of Truth. Others, like myself (Janice), see the review of the disclosure draft as an important part of advocating for your needs by requesting modifications to documents that violate your requests. However, if the Partner I'm guiding does not want to be the last to know what the betrayal history is, then I willingly shift to meet her needs. In that case, we walk into the Rite side by side and learn the history together. So, ask yourself what your preference is regarding your guide screening the disclosure document. If this is important to you, make sure you clarify these issues *before* choosing your guide.

8. **How much flexibility does the prospective guide have to do what you want and need?**
   Similar to the last issue to consider: How much flexibility do you want and need from a disclosure guide? Is your prospective disclosure guide willing to be flexible with your unique needs? Our belief is that your spouse's hidden sexual behaviors took power from you, and that the disclosure helps to provide you with what was taken: choice. So, we typically give a lot of choice to you - the location and time for the Rite of Truth, types of information requested, the ability to ask follow-up questions, pacing in the Rite of Truth, etc. How much choice does your prospective guide grant you?

9. **What is your budget and what are the costs?**

    This is an important issue to consider. In a perfect world, this process would be free. However, for the process to be most effective, we have often found it best to have a separate disclosure guide for both you and your spouse. The time spent preparing each of you for the disclosure and conducting the disclosure can be costly. What is your budget, and will this disclosure process fit within your budget? Though it can be difficult to predict exactly how many hours you'll need to prepare and also how many hours you'll need to do the Rite of Truth and post-disclosure session(s), you can absolutely ask your prospective guides what their projected costs are, given your unique situation.

    Sometimes having a couple guide who meets all your guide selection criteria, can cut cost as well as simplify the logistics of coordinating the schedules of two busy guides. Having one person who understands both sides of the FD equation eliminates snafus that occur due to miscommunication or unintended power struggles between your guides. There will be an added advantage if this professional will also be guiding your coupleship after the disclosure. However, note that having one guide can be a drawback in managing emotions during the Rite if both of you are in high distress simultaneously. If you are considering a single guide, make sure to ask how s/he will handle that situation.

10. **If you don't have local options for disclosure guides, what about an intensive?**

    If you can't find a good option locally, you may consider doing a disclosure intensive. Sometimes going to a multi-day intensive may also be a cost-effective way of containing your budget. There are a number of skilled guides who offer a several-day disclosure intensive. In this intensive option, you travel to a specific location to complete all the components of the disclosure, returning back to your area to do the aftercare work on your relationship. In choosing among intensive options, it will be important that you consider all the selection criteria we have discussed for your intensive guide. Remember to be thorough and ask about the specific staff member who would be guiding your disclosure if you are researching a larger facility. Remember that not all intensive facilitators are equal. There can be a significant difference among different staff members within the same facility. Find out how much actual experience the guide has facilitating disclosure intensives as well as running a cross-check on all of the previously listed factors.

    Please be aware that we discourage disclosure intensives when one or both parties are in severe denial about the sexual betrayal, are in active addiction, have a history of domestic violence, are suicidal, are severely dysregulated, or have any mental or physical health issue that is currently poorly managed.

Finally, when considering an intensive option, particularly if you are considering an intensive that utilizes a verbal disclosure when you are very new to the recovery process, re-read Misconception 3 in section 2, as well as our section on verbal disclosures in section 3. We believe adequate preparation is invaluable to the success of a full disclosure and that the expertise of the guide is a more critical factor for verbal disclosures. Note that the exercises in this workbook series are designed to allow you to begin your preparation prior to an intensive as a means of maximizing the gains that you can receive using that format.

WHAT DOES A RITE OF TRUTH LOOK LIKE?

Now that we have explored selecting a good disclosure guide, we want to talk briefly about what you may expect the Rite of Truth to look like (i.e., the actual ritual where you are receiving the information contained in the disclosure document). Disclosure Rites of Truth work best when following a general structure. Your specific Rite will be adapted to meet your own unique needs or the protocol of your specific guides. If you're using a written disclosure based on these disclosure workbooks, think of the Rite as having 3 main segments. In phase 1, your spouse will read his acting-out history and any questions you asked him to include from his prepared document. The next part serves as a half-time for you and your spouse to process emotional reactions and prepare to transition to the conclusion phase. Finally, phase 2 involves you asking follow-up questions about the information that was shared or clarifying the truth about suspicions and fears for events that were not addressed in the prepared document. Figure 7 gives you a snapshot of what these phases entail.

Structure for Rite of Truth

Phase 1	Reading of disclosure document
Half-time	Dealing with emotions Preparing for inquiry
Phase 2	Partner inquiry

Figure 7

Phase 1: Reading of the Disclosure Document

The disclosure day generally begins with the respective guides touching base with each of you to ensure you are prepared to begin the Rite. This might involve dealing with last minute emotions, running through anticipated coping plans, and dealing with any final preparations prior to beginning the actual Rite. This is usually done privately with your respective guides. When both of you are ready, you will then typically come back together to begin the Rite of Truth. We recommend that you determine where you feel safest to do the Rite of Truth, and how you will be entering and leaving that space. We will help you plan for this in the pages to come.

As you come together, your guide(s) may share a few words of encouragement or review the Rite guidelines. Alternatively, you and your spouse might choose to open with a statement or ritual that reminds you of the goal of moving into truth. The heart of phase 1, however, will be your spouse reading the prepared written document to you. You will likely be asked to refrain from follow-up questions at this time, other than those that help you anchor the history in time, e.g., "Are you talking about when we lived on Main Street?" or correctly comprehend the information presented, e.g., "Can you please speak louder, slower, repeat the last sentence," etc. Note that this is NOT with the intent of restricting you, but rather to create a sense of containment that allows the information in the document to unfold differently than in the staggered disclosures that have typically occurred up to this point. Any time you choose to take notes or a memo about follow-up questions you wish to ask, your spouse will be asked to pause and allow you to take the time you need.

Half-Time

Most Rites of Truth will have a break before transitioning to the Partner inquiry phase. Half-time typically involves processing any emotional reactivity from Phase 1 and putting coping plans in motion. You commonly have to deal with a range of experiences, such as shock, anger, fear, and grief. Your spouse may need to contend with fear, anger, resentment, or shame responses. This break is typically done separately, which gives one extra benefit for having two disclosure guides present in your Rite.

You may require a longer break in order to review the disclosure document, if access has been provided, determine if your questions have been adequately answered, and decide if additional questions are necessary after hearing the disclosure statement.

Phase 2: Partner Inquiry

Once you have evaluated the purpose, potential consequences, and corresponding coping plans for the potential answers to any additional questions you need to know, the Rite transitions to phase 2, the Partner inquiry phase. If all, or most, of your clarifying questions were adequately answered in the disclosure document, this phase may be brief. If, however, the document revealed deception previously unknown to you or you need more information to understand the greater context of the betrayals, then the inquiry may take quite a while.

Once this phase comes to a close, your guides will likely review immediate aftercare coping plans to make sure that no changes are necessary and plans are ready to activate. In some settings there may be follow-up processing if needed; in others, the follow-up processing may occur on a day after the Rite of Truth, but preferably as soon as possible.

Regardless of the phase of the Rite, the primary tasks for each of you are to step into truth and to conduct yourselves in a way that honors both your own and your spouse's healing. In doing so, you both reflect the spirit and intent of the disclosure - repairing your relationship foundation. Now let's examine what kind of a disclosure you should choose.

WHAT KIND OF A DISCLOSURE SHOULD WE CHOOSE?

Review the different types of disclosures in *Our Personal Relationship Disaster* section in section 3. After reviewing that section, answer the following questions. Talk through your disclosure options and where you fall on the continuum with your disclosure guide(s) to make sure you are choosing the most appropriate disclosure for your needs.

1. **How long has it been since the initial discovery/disclosure of your sexual betrayal?**
    ☐ Less than 3 months
    ☐ 3 – 6 months
    ☐ 6 months – 1 year
    ☐ 1 year – 3 years
    ☐ More than 3 years

2. **What type of recovery has your spouse undergone surrounding his sexual betrayal (check all that apply)?**
    ☐ Dealing with it on his own or with a few friends, whom he reaches out to as he deems necessary
    ☐ 12-step program or other structured support group attendance (not specific to sexual compulsivity)
    ☐ 12-step program or other structured support group attendance (related to sexual compulsivity)
    ☐ Actively working the 12-steps with a sponsor or actively working through the structured program associated with his group
    ☐ Coaching (individual or couples coaching, not with a sexual compulsivity specialist)
    ☐ Coaching (individual or couples coaching, with a sexual compulsivity specialist)
    ☐ Therapy (individual or couples counseling, not with a sexual compulsivity specialist)
    ☐ Therapy (individual or couples counseling, with a sexual compulsivity specialist)
    ☐ Working with a betrayal trauma specialist (who may also be a sexual compulsivity specialist) to help build sobriety and also restore relational healing

3. **What type of recovery have you undergone surrounding betrayal trauma (check all that apply)?**
    ☐ Dealing with it on my own or with a few friends, whom I reach out to as I deem necessary
    ☐ 12-step program or other structured support group attendance (not specific to sexual betrayal)
    ☐ 12-step program or other structured support group attendance (related to sexual betrayal)

☐ Actively working the 12-steps with a sponsor or actively working through the structured program associated with my group

☐ Coaching (individual or couples coaching, not with a sexual compulsivity specialist)

☐ Coaching (individual or couples coaching, with a sexual compulsivity specialist)

☐ Therapy (individual or couples counseling, not with a sexual compulsivity specialist)

☐ Therapy (individual or couples counseling, with a sexual compulsivity specialist)

☐ Working with a Partner betrayal trauma specialist (who may also be a sexual compulsivity specialist) to help build sobriety and also restore relational healing

4. **Check any of the following statements that apply to your situation:**

☐ I have reason to suspect that my children, family, or myself may be in danger in the presence of my spouse if we wait 6-8+ weeks for a full disclosure

☐ I have reason to suspect that the legal system may be imminently involved based on my spouse's sexual activities

☐ My financial security is severely jeopardized, or my financial security may be severely compromised if I wait for a full disclosure

☐ I have reason to believe the history of betrayals will be exposed publicly and need to stay ahead of the revelations

☐ I have reason to be concerned that I may have been exposed to sexually-transmitted diseases

☐ I have other safety concerns that I need answered ASAP. Those safety concerns include:

_____

_____

_____

_____

5. **Are you planning on doing a disclosure in an intensive format (e.g., a structured multi-day intensive where you need to do minimal preparation before the intensive)?**

☐ Yes

☐ No

☐ I am planning on an intensive, but I will begin the preparation before I arrive

6. Although anxiety-inducing, are you able to wait 6-8+ weeks for the preparation of a full disclosure document?
   - ☐ Yes
   - ☐ No
   - ☐ Unsure

7. **Do you have reason to believe that your disclosure preparation will take LONGER than 6-8 weeks to prepare? If so, are you willing to wait longer than this? Make sure to talk to your disclosure guide about the time frame you are wanting for your disclosure.**
   - ☐ **Yes**
   - ☐ **No**
   - ☐ **Unsure**

8. **Do you suspect that you already know a significant percentage of the facts about your spouse's sexual betrayal?**
   - ☐ **Yes**
   - ☐ **No**

9. **What are you primarily needing from the FD (check the answer that best fits your needs):**
   - ☐ Just the facts of his sexual betrayal
   - ☐ Validation of my pain as a result of my spouse's sexual betrayal
   - ☐ Both the facts and validation of my pain as a result of my spouse's sexual betrayal, but I can tolerate having less validation at this time if the facts are revealed.
   - ☐ Both the facts and validation of my pain as a result of my spouse's sexual betrayal, I'm willing to wait until he has developed greater emotional maturity in his recovery to receive validation and empathy.

10. **Your situation is unique (check all the answers that apply)**
    - ☐ One party doesn't want disclosure
    - ☐ The relationship is ending
    - ☐ Finances limit your options for FD
    - ☐ You have limited access to trained professionals
    - ☐ Medical or mental health issues may impact FD decisions

Now look at your results. Match your results with what disclosure seems most appropriate to you and your relationship at this time. Make sure to talk through your responses with your disclosure guide(s), particularly if you and your spouse have different responses for this section. Look again at the *Disclosure on the Continuum* graphic in Figure 8 below. Circle where you believe you are on the continuum, and then read So *Which Disclosure is Right for Us?* in the next section to determine which disclosure is right for you.

Disclosure Continuum

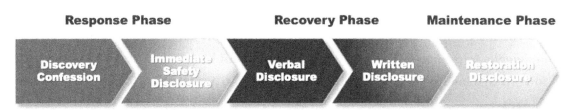

Figure 4

SO WHICH DISCLOSURE IS RIGHT FOR US?

Going It Alone:

On *Question 2* or *Question 3*, if you only checked dealing with it alone, that indicates either you or your spouse has no recovery structure. Planning a FD at this point would be like jumping out of a plane without a parachute; you might survive the landing but the damage would likely be irreparable. Use the information in this book to find guides who will help you create a recovery foundation. Then begin the active preparation for your FD.

Immediate Safety Disclosure:

On *Question 1*, if you said you were less than 6 months post-discovery or post initial disclosure, **AND** you had significant safety concerns checked in Question 4, an immediate safety disclosure may be appropriate for you and your situation. Talk with your disclosure guide to determine if this type of disclosure makes sense for what you are needing right now. Note the benefits and risks that we mentioned above for doing an immediate safety disclosure. Turn to Appendix 1 for more information about doing an immediate safety disclosure.

Verbal Disclosure:

On *Question 1*, if you said you were less than 6 months post-discovery or post initial disclosure, OR you are planning on attending a disclosure intensive that does not require much pre-intensive preparation *(Question 5)*, **OR** you have reason to believe your spouse's willingness to more fully disclose may be spontaneous and fleeting and the motivation may only occur as a result of the momentum built in the moment of opportunity, then a verbal disclosure may be right for you. You may opt for a verbal disclosure if you aren't able to wait for a full written disclosure document to be created or you do not believe your spouse can tolerate the sustained effort to create a written document. Note the benefits and risks that we mentioned above for doing a verbal disclosure and talk about this option with your disclosure guide(s).

Written Disclosure:

On *Question 7*, if you stated that you are able to wait for a full written disclosure to be completed, a written disclosure may be right for you. The remainder of this workbook series will help prepare you for a Full Disclosure in a written format. For a full written disclosure, you may be at any point after the initial discovery/disclosure of sexual betrayal *(Question 1)*. You also may be in any phase of the recovery process *(Question 2 and Question 3)*. A written disclosure could be done in an intensive setting or in a regular "outpatient" setting (Question

5), and this type of disclosure could be completed whether or not you believe you know all or most of the facts of your spouse's sexual betrayal *(Question 8)*. A written disclosure will inform you of the facts of your spouse's sexual betrayal, often as a prerequisite for building further validation for your pain *(Question 9)*. Please note the benefits and risks of doing a written disclosure and talk about these with your disclosure guide(s).

Restoration Disclosure:

On *Question 1*, if you said you were at least 1 year after the initial discovery/disclosure of sexual betrayal, AND on *Question 2*, if your spouse is in good recovery (attendance AND participation in recovery-related activities as well as relationship-restoring activities), AND on Question 9, you said that you are looking for validation of your pain in addition to facts, AND a Full Disclosure of the facts has already taken place, then a validating or other Restoration Disclosure may be right for you. Please note that a Restoration Disclosure should only be done if you and your spouse are ready for such a disclosure. You can determine readiness by a combination of having been in the healing process for a while *(Question 1)*, if your spouse is in good recovery and can be empathetic to your pain *(Question 2)*, a Full Disclosure has already occurred or will occur as part of the restoration process, and your spouse has shown growth in the ability to validate and empathize with your emotions *(Question 9)*. Talk to your disclosure guide(s) to determine if you are ready for a validating or other Restoration Disclosure. Though we recognize that a Restoration Disclosure is an important part of healing for you and your relationship, we also know that many couples need time to be ready for such a disclosure. That's why we're focusing here in this disclosure workbook on a written disclosure. By going through a written disclosure, you will receive a Full Disclosure of facts, truth will give you a foundation of healing as you prepare for the deeper empathy journey in the future.

Unique Situations:

If you checked any of the items on *Question 10*, review the information in Appendix 3.

SECTION FIVE:
CONSIDERATIONS ABOUT TRUTH

THE USE OF POLYGRAPHS IN THE DISCLOSURE PROCESS

Now that we've talked about unique situations in the disclosure process, it is time to address a controversial topic: doing disclosures with or without a polygraph.

We could write a whole book on the use of polygraphs and how they can be incorporated into disclosures. We can't get into all the details about a polygraph, or the ethics of using them, but we do want to say here that polygraphs are more and more frequently used in conjunction with Full Disclosures. Why? The polygraph assists in eliciting and validating truth. And since the purpose of a FD is full and complete truth, many have found it helpful to use polygraphs as an accountability tool for disclosures. Polygraphs can also help your spouse learn what truth is, perhaps for the first time. As such, they can serve as a bridge toward trust repair and assist in building a foundation of truth and honesty in your relationship.

What about false positives and false negatives? We do recognize that these are a possibility. A simple internet search on polygraphs will show that polygraphs aren't "perfect." Yet we also know that though there is NO "perfect" tool, polygraphs can be helpful in securing a foundation of truth in a disclosure setting. The point of using a polygraph is not to punish your spouse, but rather to restore a sense of trust and safety in the truth being validated through this instrument.

There are two main components of your spouse for taking the polygraph exam: first, is his willingness to take the polygraph, and second, is telling the truth on the exam. His willingness to take a polygraph will demonstrate to you that he is invested in your healing and safety and is willing to go to whatever lengths it takes to restore trust. If he refuses to take a polygraph, it will communicate to you that he is not willing to go to whatever lengths necessary and it may even appear as though he is hiding truth from you.

Benefits of Using a Polygraph for Your Disclosure

In two APSATS surveys, 76% of Partners and 73.6% of Disclosers report that the benefits of a polygraph outweigh any harms. In addition, 73% of Disclosers rated a polygraph as part of the FD process as helpful, with 60% rating it as extremely helpful. In a corresponding APSATS survey of Partners, 72.5% rated it as helpful, with 56% rating it as extremely helpful.[12]

As you can see, the majority of respondents, BOTH Partners and Disclosers, who have gone through a polygraph have found the process helpful. Just as most of us would be extra cautious in filing our taxes if we knew for sure we are going to be audited, we have found that your spouse will tend to work harder and write his disclosure document more completely when a polygraph is involved. Without one, you will be relying on his document being written on the honor system. As you well know, though, you need more than his words to rebuild trust. The polygraph has the added benefit to your Rite of Truth of providing an external method of checking on deception.

For you, a polygraph serves as a support tool to reinforce the truth of the information you are hearing in the FD. It can also prevent future staggered disclosures that may re-traumatize you by increasing your spouse's motivation for FULL disclosure. This instrument lines up words with reality, and it can be one more tool that helps you recalibrate your intuition.

A polygraph can also assist in rapidly breaking through your spouse's denial and lies. Additionally, it provides an accountability inspiration to help NOT withhold any information in his disclosure document. And since nobody's memory is perfect, should he remember further information after the FD, a polygraph reinforces that this information was truly forgotten and not intentionally withheld.

For your relationship, a polygraph can help reinforce the foundation of truth he is building. This reinforced truth builds safety and enhances trust. Polygraphs can also be used as an ongoing support tool in relationships to affirm continuing truth in your relationship.

When to Use a Polygraph

If you and your spouse do choose to use a fidelity polygraph as part of your FD, you will need to determine if you'd like to use one before and/or after the Rite of Truth. There are pros and cons for each option, and the option you choose will impact the flow of your preparation as well as the flow of the Rite of Truth.

A polygraph **before** the Rite helps assure that the disclosure document is complete and truthful. This offers the important benefit of preventing you from going through a painful Rite that is based on a deceptive disclosure statement. Having this polygraph option prior to the Rite of Truth gives you the choice to opt in or out of the Rite of Truth depending on his polygraph results.

A polygraph before the Rite will require you to develop a complete set of all the questions you need addressed in the disclosure document sooner rather than later. You will be working on getting complete and thorough disclosure questions to your spouse or his guide as soon as possible, so that the answers to those questions can be written into the disclosure document prior to the polygraph. Your disclosure guide will also be helping you to develop polygraph questions in a format that can be tested on a polygraph (e.g., fact-based questions as opposed to emotionally-focused, heart-based questions). Once the polygraph has been passed, then the Rite of Truth can be scheduled. See Volume Two for more information on developing polygraph questions.

Since your questions may change dramatically after he has shared his disclosure document in the Rite, this option may require a second polygraph if questions arise that you didn't anticipate prior to the disclosure.

A fidelity polygraph **after** the Rite of Truth addresses deception in both the written document and any follow-up clarifying questions you may want to ask during the Rite. This option takes away some of the time pressure for you to anticipate any questions you might have before the Rite, as you can ask questions after the disclosure document is read that may arise spontaneously during the Rite itself. However, if your spouse does not pass a polygraph question after the Rite, you run the risk of having put yourself through a painful and potentially re-traumatizing experience. A failed polygraph question after the Rite may also cast a shadow on truthful information that your spouse shared over the ENTIRE disclosure process.

The specifics of how many questions the polygraph examiner includes and who gets to determine what the questions are varies from region to region and examiner to examiner. However, some version of, "Did you lie?" and "Did you intentionally leave a sexual betrayal out?" will be included.

Both authors of this workbook are familiar with using the polygraph as a tool for disclosure, Dan more with exams that occur before the Rite and Janice more with those that come after. We don't take a stance on which method is preferred because your situation is unique, and one size doesn't fit all. In general, we have seen the fidelity polygraph to be a helpful, although not foolproof, tool in the disclosure process.

The Use of Follow-up Polygraphs

Lastly, we mentioned previously that a polygraph can be used as a follow-up tool for helping to rebuild trust. Some couples have found it helpful to do follow-up polygraphs, particularly for a time after the disclosure. A 3-month or 6-month post-disclosure polygraph acts like a security system in your house: It provides a sense of security that the foundation repair begun in the FD will continue after the process is over. It can serve as an accountability tool to help your spouse maintain his work in his program. Similarly, post-disclosure polygraphs can serve as a safety net to help bolster your sense of safety after the disclosure. Doubts, fears, and further questions can be verified later through a polygraph, allowing you to focus more intently on healing.

Whether you use the polygraph as a one-time part of the FD or continue to use it as part of an ongoing recovery program, its helpfulness to you will boil down to three things: the accuracy of any given test, your spouse's willingness to step into truth, and how you use the polygraph to help your recovery and your relationship. The Discloser version of this workbook encourages your spouse that if he is going through this disclosure process and is going to add a fidelity polygraph, that he be 100% forthright. He runs the risk of damaging you more by going through this process deceptively than if he were not to go through it at all. If you and your spouse decide to include a polygraph in your disclosure process, we cannot caution you enough about NOT viewing the polygraph as the sole basis for your sense of relational safety moving forward. It is merely one tool that can be used in recovery. In fact, we caution you against relying on any one tool. That said, we have seen the benefit of using a fidelity polygraph in our practices and encourage you to consider if using one for your disclosure process would be something that would help your spouse build a stronger foundation of trust based on truth.

Ultimately, we recognize that the use of polygraphs is a controversial topic. We recommend that you talk through the specifics of using or not using a polygraph for the unique needs of your coupleship with a qualified professional.

Be aware that the fidelity polygraph process is quite different from a standard polygraph. Those who are seasoned examiners are familiar with the disclosure process and often prefer to work in conjunction with your guide team. We also strongly recommend that you do not hire a polygraph examiner directly without involvement of your disclosure guide(s) through every phase of the FD. This will ensure a more successful disclosure process.

SHOULD WE INCLUDE A POLYGRAPH?

Let's consider the use of using a fidelity polygraph for your particular situation. If you and your spouse are firmly opposed to even considering the use of a polygraph to assist in this process, then you can skip to the next section, A Final Note About Truth. If, however, you aren't sure or if the two of you have different opinions, then we encourage you to read further. The information is meant to dispel some fears, address some pros and cons, and offer options in making this decision.

Before addressing this, however, we acknowledge that we are biased on this issue. We have found, in general, the polygraph to be a helpful tool. Neither of us requires its use, but in most cases, we do see positive results when it has been used. Despite its overall helpful results, we acknowledge it is not a perfect tool and reiterate that it should NEVER be used as the sole index of recovery progress.

Let's look at some common concerns you may have about taking the polygraph:

Concern 1:
If we need something like a polygraph to help build trust, then what is the point of even being in a relationship?

This concern is understandable, but the reality is that you are already in a relationship that needs help to rebuild trust. Rebuilding trust after betrayal will be a long, difficult journey for the two of you, particularly if the betrayal was packaged with lies and manipulation over an extended period of time. The fidelity polygraph is simply a tool that can shorten the journey by helping to confirm that what is shared during the FD is the complete truth.

Concern 2:
A fidelity polygraph treats the Discloser like a criminal.

A fidelity polygraph is a different type of procedure than a criminal polygraph. Good, experienced fidelity examiners understand the importance of the Full Disclosure process and go out of their way to make sure your spouse isn't treated like a criminal. Their goal is for truth to come out to aid in the disclosure process. They aren't conducting the exam to help either the prosecution or defense at a trial, so they don't have a hidden agenda about someone passing or failing

Concern 3:
Anxiety will cause the examinee to fail.

Experienced fidelity examiners work to mitigate nervousness and are trained to take this into account in evaluating the responses.

Concern 4:
The examiner wants their examinee to fail.

Good examiners don't want their clients to fail; they want them to tell the truth, the whole truth, and nothing but the truth. They use the polygraph as a tool to motivate honesty and to detect deception if the client is not willing to be completely honest.

Concern 5:
Since no polygraph is 100% accurate, the examinee could fail a question when actually telling the truth.

It is a realistic concern that polygraphs are not 100% accurate and it needs to be taken into consideration when deciding if you are going to use one. There are a number of different techniques that have been validated. Accuracy varies depending on the technique used; however, according to the American Polygraph Association the decision accuracy rate across the validated techniques is 87%.[13] Even though the overall accuracy is quite high, we recognize that some individuals may fall into that remaining 13%.[14]

In our survey of disclosing parties,[15] we found that those who responded to our survey shared the same fear about polygraphs not being 100% accurate. Yet out of all of the respondents to our survey, none of the Disclosers reported failing questions when they were actually telling the truth. In fact, 15.8% of the respondents said they were lying when taking the polygraph, and the polygraph caught their lies.

The implication is that without the use of the polygraph, you will have to rely on being a human lie detector. So, in factoring the risk you will need to ask yourself, which lie detector, the polygraph or being a human lie detector, will be the greater risk? As one of the Partners in our survey stated, "It is not 100% infallible but it can provide the push an addict needs to get 100% honest."[16]

Concern 6:
Since no polygraph is 100% accurate, the examinee could pass a question when actually lying.

That is another realistic fear. In assessing the risks, you will again need to compare the odds for the polygraph vs. human lie detector to determine which one will help you and your spouse move forward in both your individual and relationship recoveries. And as we shared in Concern 5, among the participants of our Discloser survey, 15.8% of them were lying in the polygraph and were caught.

Concern 7:
Since what is at stake is so high, the Discloser is risking a lot by taking a polygraph. Therefore, not taking that risk avoids potential harm for him.

It is true that by not taking the polygraph your spouse avoids some potential harm. However, by not cooperating with a polygraph, all the risk is shifted to you. Don't make a decision about the polygraph based solely on potential harm, because there will be the potential for harm either way. The question then becomes: who is going to bear the burden of that risk? Him or you?

Concern 8:
Not being able to remember an event will cause a failed polygraph question.

It is not true that not being able to remember an event will result in a failed polygraph. If an examinee has no memory for an event, he or she will deny the behavior and pass the question on the polygraph because they truly do not remember the event. This is not a problem of deception; this is a problem of memory. The polygraph does not test memory, it tests the examinee's conviction about the truth. Genuine memory problems will affect the disclosure document itself in the same fashion.

This is the reason why many professionals suggest that in a perfect world the Rite of Truth and accompanying polygraphs wait until at least 3 months of sobriety have been achieved. There are a number of brain processes that begin to shift at around 3 months sober.[16] One outcome of those shifts is that it sometimes results in access to memories that previously were blocked. This is why there is an exercise in Volume Two of this workbook series that asks you to develop boundaries, or a protocol, for what to do if excavated memories are recovered after the disclosure or polygraph process is over. As we stated above, however, we also know that some couples will need to go through this process before 3 months of continued sobriety have been completed and will need to factor this into their expectations of the process. This sobriety period may be one factor to consider in your decision on the timing of FD.

Remember that your spouse will be sharing his history of sexual behaviors to the best of his awareness at this time. The point of the polygraph is to determine if the information given truly IS to the best of his knowledge, or if he is still INTENTIONALLY withholding and/or lying about some pieces of information.

Concern 9:
I don't know how to determine whether a polygraph examiner is experienced at conducting fidelity disclosure polygraphs.

It can be difficult to find a good fidelity polygraph examiner, so often the easiest route is to make sure your guide is involved in the selection of the polygraph examiner. Your guide will further help you screen the examiner to see he or she is a good fit for your needs. According to fidelity polygraph examiner Dianne Robinson,[17] who has over 34-years of experience at conducting fidelity polygraphs, you need to ask questions of the examiner to make sure they are familiar with disclosure types of exams as well as with working closely with therapists. Specifically ask if the examiner is willing to work with you in coming up with the questions.

Concern 10:
There are no experienced fidelity polygraph examiners near me, so we don't have the option of a polygraph as part of our disclosure process.

It is not necessarily true that if there are no experienced polygraph examiners near you, you can't use a polygraph as part of your disclosure. The regulations around polygraph exams, including whether and how they are used in the legal system, vary from state to state and region to region. In some areas there are a lot of choices for examiners, in others none at all. The authors of this workbook are grateful to live in areas with lots of options, so we have the luxury of having many choices, including being able to work with examiners who are extremely experienced in conducting fidelity disclosure polygraphs. We often have clients travel to us to complete the polygraph in a multi-day disclosure intensive. Although there are drawbacks to completing your FD in an intensive format, they can bypass some of the logistical problems of coordinating among local guides and be a godsend for those living in areas with no professionals who specialize in FDs, no fidelity polygraph examiners, and/or no access to a supportive recovery community.

Alternatively, many people work with local professional guides for the FD but travel outside of their own geographical area to complete the polygraph with an experienced examiner. This may be inconvenient. However, if you have a good relationship with your disclosure guide(s) and a strong recovery support community with peers who have been through the FD process, then this might be the best option for you.

For those of you interested in including a polygraph, remember that this will influence the flow and pace at which you prepare for your FD. Should you decide to use a fidelity polygraph, there will be additional information to assist you with this in upcoming exercises in Volume Two.

References:

[12]*Association of Partners of Sex Addicts Trauma Specialists. (2019). APSATS Multidimensional Partner Trauma Model Training: Module 4: Disclosure Trauma. Cincinnati, OH: Independently Published.*

[13]*H Gougler, M. Nelson, R, Handler, M., Krapohl, D., Shaw, P., and Bierma, L. (2010-2011) Meta-Analytic Survey of Criterion Accuracy of Validated Polygraph Techniques: Report Prepared for The American Polygraph Association Board of Directors.*

[14]*Hang in There Buddy Disclosure Survey (2018).*

[15]*Hold on Sister Partner Disclosure Survey (2018). Comments used with permission..*

[16]*Dr. Jill Manning, e-mail message to author, March 3, 2018.*

[17]*Dianne Robinson, e-mail message to author, January 7, 2019.*

A FINAL NOTE ABOUT TRUTH

Before moving to the disclosure preparation exercises in this workbook, we want to educate you about two types of information, two types of truth that the FD will reveal – **Content Truth** and **Behavioral Truth**. We would like to acknowledge the influence of Doug Weiss, PhD on the development of this concept of content and behavioral truth during multiple communications with Janice.

Content truth focuses on the accuracy of facts, the content of what will be disclosed. For your spouse, that task is simple: tell the truth by sharing the facts. For you, preparation for content truth involves a thorough examination of what you need to know, carefully differentiating the level of detail you may *want* to know when emotionally triggered from what you actually *need* to know to continue in your own healing. In essence, this means determining what level of detail you need to know about the betrayal facts.

However, our behavior also tells us something about truth, and sometimes it speaks the more important truth. If your spouse says he is taking full responsibility for his actions but then proceeds to minimize, justify or blame others for his decisions, his behavior contradicts his verbal claim. In this case, the behavioral truth speaks louder than the content that is shared. For him, the task is to prepare a coping plan for dealing with potential defensiveness, resentment, shame, or other strong emotions that could dishonor the disclosure process. More importantly, during the Rite of Truth, the task is to put the coping plan into motion if needed. This might mean taking a time out to calm down when feeling frustrated or asking for a few moments to collect himself. The behavioral truth in this scenario is that he is learning to use his recovery tools and, as a consequence, is growing in emotional maturity. This will be incredibly important information for you because truthful facts without maturity will not lead to a sense of security that he is becoming trustworthy.

Likewise, in preparing for the FD, your task is to develop a coping plan to help you better deal with the level of detail you have asked for. Before the Rite, that means such things as facing your fears about what the truth might be, confronting anger, accepting the reality of the pain that will come with truth being revealed, and using the exercises in Volume Two of this workbook series to build an emotional safety net to help hold you up during and after the FD. During the Rite, it means a willingness to put your coping plan into motion. This might include things such as requesting a time out to cry, scream, or allow yourself to shake in fear as long as needed; or perhaps taking notes if your brain is having trouble keeping up with the information that is being shared. It also means restraining the impulse to interrupt with additional questions or accusations before the inquiry phase – the willingness to listen to the disclosure you have asked your spouse to prepare. We can see a depiction of content and behavioral truth shown in Figure 9:

Content and Behavioral Truth

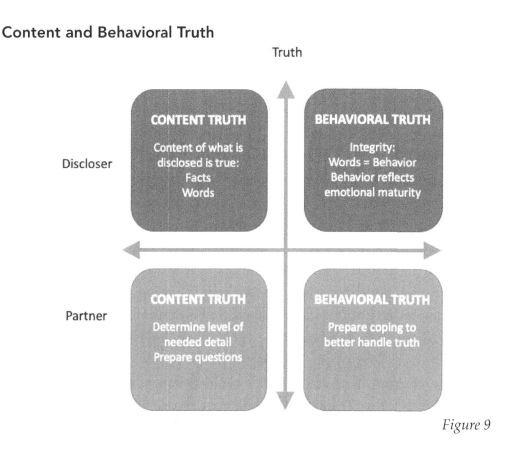

Figure 9

In addition to helping you prepare for the content truth aspects of your Rite of Truth, workbook Volume Two and your guides will help you prepare for and honor the process by managing your emotions and behavior during the Rite. Remember that the choreography of the Rite of Truth is different with different guides, so you will want to ask your specific guides what the Rite looks like for the FD's they facilitate, as well as how they will help you prepare for content and behavioral truth.

SUMMARY

We hope Volume One has been helpful to you in understanding more about the Full Disclosure process and how it can help you, and your relationship, heal. Our intent was to inform you about the purpose, nature, and choice points for disclosures on the continuum so you could decide if this would be of benefit in your recovery.

For those of the brave women and men who have decided that a Full Disclosure is necessary for repairing the foundation of your intimacy pyramid, Volume Two of this 3 volume series is a step-by-step guide in preparing for your Rite of Truth, while your spouse's workbook will shepherd him through creating the disclosure document that restores truth to your relationship foundation.

Volume Three will help hold you up after the Rite as you empower yourself with truth, make some important boundary decisions about your relationship, and begin to rebuild your intimacy pyramid. Volume Three for you spouse is the beginning of his step-by-step journey of developing and deepening compassion and empathy for the impact of his betrayals on you.

It will be a difficult journey, but one in which the gains will be well worth the pain.

We wish you all the best,
Janice and Dan

Appendices

APPENDIX 1

Conducting an Immediate Safety Disclosure

If discovery or initial disclosure occurred recently, and if you have significant safety concerns, an Immediate Safety Disclosure maybe right for you.

Please note, this immediate safety disclosure is NOT to take the place of a full disclosure if you'd like the FD. Instead, the point of an immediate safety disclosure is to provide a base level of safety to better help you wait for the full disclosure. By having answers for a few safety questions immediately, such a disclosure can give you some basic reassurance around important safety concerns.

If you've determined that an immediate safety disclosure is right for you, first review the following items and place a check next to any of the following sentences that apply:

☐ I have reason to suspect that my children, family, or myself may be in danger in the presence of my spouse if I wait 6-8+ weeks for a full disclosure

☐ I have reason to suspect that the legal system may be imminently involved based upon my spouse's sexual activities

☐ My financial security is severely jeopardized, or my financial security may be severely compromised if I wait for a full disclosure

☐ I have reason to believe the history of betrayals will be exposed publicly and need to stay ahead of the revelations

☐ I have other safety concern(s) that I need answered as soon as possible. Those safety concern(s) include:

_____

_____

_____

_____

Talk to your disclosure guide to make sure an immediate safety disclosure is right for you. If you've decided that such a disclosure is needed right now, consider the following procedure:

1. **Consider if you will use a polygraph.**

   First, consider if you are going to use a polygraph for this immediate safety disclosure. We often recommend the use of a polygraph for such disclosures, as they can help reinforce the truth that is shared in these disclosures.

   If you are going to use a polygraph, set aside the appropriate dates as soon as possible. To avoid scheduling delays, you want to begin setting a schedule with your polygraph examiner immediately. Also, decide if you'd like to do a polygraph before or after the safety disclosure.

   * For additional resources about including a fidelity polygraph as part of a FD, see Volume Two of Full Disclosure: Seeking Truth after Sexual Betrayal.

2. **Write specific questions you'd like answered for this immediate safety disclosure.**

   Use the possible safety concerns you checked above as a guide to help you write these questions. As you write your questions, make sure they are specific and behavioral. You want to make sure the questions are as clear as possible and behavioral, since that is what a polygraph can test.

   Polygraphs will not accurately test thoughts or ideas. So for example, if you have concerns for the safety of your children, you can ask a question such as, "Have you ever sexually touched or engaged in any form of sexual contact with any of our children?" as opposed to, "Are our children safe?" Be as clear and specific as possible.

   Again, remember that an immediate safety disclosure is NOT a full disclosure. You will have an opportunity to ask more questions later. For now, the point is to get answers to a question or a few questions that you need answered right now to give you safety while you wait until the FD. Write down any specific questions you need answered right now to give you that basic sense of safety:

   _____

   _____

   _____

3. **Review your questions with your disclosure guide(s) and, if necessary, review them with your polygraph examiner.**

   Review your questions with your disclosure guide(s). Your guide can help you format questions in a more behavioral way if you are having trouble doing so. They can also help you think through what types of questions, if any, to ask during this session.

   If you are stuck, you may consider asking your polygraph examiner to word questions. Because they are experts at administering polygraphs, they will have an idea on how to most effectively word your questions.

4. **Schedule your immediate safety disclosure session.**

   Now that you've written down your questions, it is time to schedule your disclosure session. The timing of this session should coincide with the polygraph if you've opted to have one.

5. **Conduct your immediate safety disclosure session.**

   You've now set the date set for the session and for your polygraph (if applicable), and you have your questions ready. It is now time to conduct your immediate safety disclosure session.

   Remember that this session is to help you get a basic sense of safety. Decide how you'd like to proceed in the following areas:

Time frame

We recommend setting aside a couple of hours for this session, depending on the results. In a best-case-scenario, none of your safety concerns will be substantiated and you may not need all the time. If any of your safety concerns are substantiated, you may need time to process and come up with a boundary plan.

Setting

Decide where you feel safest conducting this session. You may be new to therapy and may have selected your disclosure guide(s) only recently. It is important to find a setting that feels as safe as possible for this session.

Boundary updating as needed

Depending on the results of this session, you may need to create some safety boundaries moving forward. Work with your disclosure guide to help create your boundaries.

6. **Review any boundary request as needed and prepare a next-steps plan.**

   After having created a plan for any additional boundaries you need, work with your disclosure guide on communicating this plan and creating a next-steps plan for the coming weeks. As you think through this plan, consider what you will need in the coming weeks to feel safe. Also consider how you'd like to proceed with the FD given the results of this immediate safety disclosure. Write down any thoughts that you have about this plan after talking with your disclosure guide:

   _____

   _____

   _____

   _____

   _____

   _____

   _____

   _____

   _____

   _____

   _____

   _____

APPENDIX 2

Resources for Selecting Your Disclosure Guide(s)

Please note that this list is comprised of organizations with which the authors have some degree of familiarity. The list is neither exhaustive, nor intended to be an endorsement of any of the organizations or professionals trained by them.

Certain certifications require therapists or coaches to receive specialized training and/or consultation supervision in treating sexual addiction or betrayal trauma; however, some require only didactic training with no period of consultation supervision in implementing the training. Some of these organizations and their current requirements include:

American Association for Sex Addiction Therapy (AASAT)
www.aasat.org
- Partner Recovery Therapist (PRT)
- Sexual Recovery Therapist (SRT)
- Intimacy Anorexia Therapist (IAT)
- Partner Betrayal Therapist (PBT)
- Partner Recovery Coach
- Sexual Recovery Coach

✓mental health professional certification ✓coaching certification
✓educational component ✓supervision required ✓disclosure included in training

Association of Partners of Sex Addicts Trauma Specialists (APSATS)
www.apsats.org
- Certified Clinical Partner Specialist (CCPS)
- Certified Partner Coach (CPC)

✓mental health professional certification ✓coaching certification
✓educational component ✓supervision required ✓disclosure included in training

Christian Sex Addiction Specialists International (C-SASI)
www.c-sasi.org
- Certified Clinical Sex Addiction Specialist (CCSAS)
- Certified Pastoral/Lay Sex Addiction Specialist (C(P/L)SAS)
- Certified Facilitator Sex Addiction Specialist (CFSAS)

- Certified Sex Addiction Specialist, Coach (CSASC)
- Pastoral Sex Addiction Professional (PSAP)

✓mental health professional certification ✓coaching certification
✓educational component ✓supervision required ✓disclosure included in training

Hope & Freedom Institute: Three-Day Disclosure Intensive Model
www.hopeandfreedom.com/sex-addiction-therapist-chfp-training
- Certified Hope and Freedom Practitioner

✓mental health professional certification ×coaching certification
✓educational component ✓supervision required ✓disclosure included in training

International Institute for Trauma and Addiction Professionals (IITAP)
www.iitap.com
- Certified Sex Addiction Therapist (CSAT)
- Pastoral Sex Addiction Professional (PSAP)

✓mental health professional certification ×coaching certification
✓educational component ✓supervision required ✓disclosure included in training

Kintsugi Recovery Partners (KRP)
www.KintsugiRecoveryPartners.com
Note that this Certified Disclosure Guide training program is currently in development.
- Certified Clinical Disclosure Guide (CCDG)
- Certified Disclosure Guide Coach (CDGC)

✓mental health professional certification ✓coaching certification
✓educational component ✓supervision required ✓disclosure included in training

Society for the Advancement of Sexual Health (SASH)
www.sash.net
- Advanced Topics in Problematic Sexual Behavior (ATPSB) – Note that this is a didactic program only, not a certification program.

×mental health professional certification ×coaching certification
✓educational component ×supervision required ✓disclosure included in training

	Didactic	Includes Disclosure	Supervision Consultation	Mental Health Professionals	Coaching
AASAT	✓	✓	✓	✓	✓
APSATS	✓	✓	✓	✓	✓
C-SASI	✓	✓	✓	✓	✓
Hope & Freedom	✓	✓	✓	✓	
IITAP	✓	✓	✓	✓	
Kintsugi Recovery Partners	✓	✓	✓	✓	✓
SASH	✓	✓		*	

*Not a certification program

APPENDIX 3

Unique Situations

If you checked that your situation is unique on the Which Disclosure is Right for Us questionnaire, we will address some unique situations that may come up in the disclosure process. For example, there are some situations where one party decides that they do not want to go through with the disclosure, other situations where the Partner decides she no longer wishes to remain in the relationship, other situations that involve financial difficulties, still others that include limited access to professional supports, situations that involve medical issues, and finally situations that involve disclosure to children. We want to first emphasize that these are all complex situations, so make sure that you talk through the intricacies of your particular situation with a professional who understands sexual compulsion and Partner betrayal trauma. This professional and your support team can help you understand the risks and benefits of going through a disclosure process if the purpose isn't for relational restoration.

Unique Situation:
One party doesn't want disclosure or the relationship is ending

In some situations, where couples want to continue healing their relationships after betrayal, some betraying spouses want to disclose their history of betrayals, but their Partners do not want to be burdened with this information. If you are in this situation, we appreciate and accept your healing choice. Yet, be aware that the intimacy foundation that you and your spouse are building will not be based on a solid foundation of full truth.

Conversely, what we have typically found is that if you need the FD and your spouse refuses to complete it, your relationship will have little chance of truly healing. In situations where the spouse is not willing to come clean, there is often a wound left open in the relationship that will not heal on its own. The long-term chances of having a deeply satisfying, emotionally-intimate relationship may diminish. Like putting broken pieces of a pottery vessel in place without sealing the cracks, you will end up with a leaky vessel, an open wound that doesn't heal.

On the other hand, sometimes relationships cannot recover after discovery of sexual betrayal. If you are in a situation where your relationship has ended or is moving toward divorce, how do you handle disclosure? We want to reiterate that FDs are intended for the purpose of relational restoration and healing. Furthermore, FDs are NOT designed to be used for any legal purposes in terms of child custody or other divorce proceedings. The types of disclosure we are advocating for here involve safety for both parties. In no way should this information be used or exploited for legal or other purposes. We can't guarantee any outcome if you are to go through a FD, yet we want to reiterate that the spirit behind going through this process is NOT to use this information to end a relationship or to gain leverage.

That said, disclosures can still be valuable for some Partners to help make sense of what happened in their relationship in order to help their own healing and further understanding for any future relationships. If your relationship is ending or has ended, your spouse may have been given the advice that telling you more information would only hurt you. Although we know that can be the case, we can also say that some Partners need to know the information, regardless of what happens to the relationship, in order to help with their own healing. In cases where the betraying party is willing to give you the information, it can help you walk away from the relationship and move forward with rebuilding your life. But do talk to your disclosure guides to determine if doing such a disclosure is right for you.

Unique Situation:
Limited finances/resources

Doing a Full Disclosure is an involved process, and it may need the support of two trained professionals. If you do not have the resources for such a disclosure, you can still make the most of a tough situation. We DO recommend that you find a professional who can support you through your FD, and that person can talk to you about creative ways to help guide you through this process. If multiple guides are not an option, you can nevertheless still receive supportive guidance to make your FD as safe as possible. For example, working with one professional who anchors you as a couple, maximizing the prep work you do outside of session, working with a pre-licensed professional under the supervision of an experienced guide and following recommendations that we have provided, and bringing them to your disclosure guide can all help streamline the process for you. We have also found that doing more work on your own between meetings with your disclosure guide(s) can dramatically reduce the cost of this process. This is one major reason we're writing this workbook – to help streamline the FD process, as well as to save you time and money.

Unique Situation:
Limited access to trained professionals

If you are in an area that is remote or doesn't have trained professionals, you may find it difficult to have the best FD possible. At times you may even know more information about disclosures than professionals in your area, and you may feel that you have to educate your chosen support person on the FD process. In these cases, we have found it helpful to find a trained coach to assist you in the disclosure preparation process. For some, working remotely via a videoconference or telephone platform can help bridge the distance. One caveat about distance work: while distance sessions can work well in the FD preparation phase, we DISCOURAGE you from conducting the Rite of Truth without your guide(s) in the same location as you are. Even well-guided Rites can register a high intensity on the emotional Richter scale. When that happens, you are going to want your response team in the same city you are, not at a remote location. We have listed some of the organizations who train professionals for guiding disclosures in Appendix 2. Finally, we, the authors, offer disclosure and post-disclosure intensives to help guide couples through this process. If you are in an area without trained professionals, this could be a powerful alternative for you.

Unique Situation:
Medical or mental health issues

Given that the average disclosure can register a high intensity of emotional pain, physical condition and medical status are key factors when considering the timing of your FD. This is true whether you or your spouse are struggling with an ongoing severe mental illness, medical illness, disability, a pain management issue that can be exacerbated or destabilized under FD stress, or if you are dealing with a more temporary condition such as pregnancy. Your guides will naturally be cautious and want you to consult with your medical doctor about the wisest choices for if and when you participate in a FD. In some cases, they may ask for a medical release from your physician to confirm that you have carefully discussed the possible medical consequences associated with participating in the FD process. We know that you might feel uncomfortable discussing this personal issue with your physician, especially if you also have to educate your doctor about the need for a FD and the relative distress of a prolonged wait versus the distress of the FD itself. However, the benefit of making a fully-informed decision far outweighs the risk of making important FD decisions without considering the impact on your physical or mental health. If you have a medical or mental health issue that may impact your FD, we strongly encourage you to seek medical advice before proceeding further with your FD preparation.

Not-So Unique Situation:
What do we tell the kids?

If you have children, it is important that they be considered in the FD decision process. Whether or not your coupleship survives, you have a lifelong relationship with your children that will be affected by your recovery, so their needs should be factored into your recovery and disclosure decisions. Additionally, some situations involve discovery of the sexual betrayal by the kids (e.g., children discovering acting-out behaviors, friends in a small community informing the children of the betrayal before their parents have, law enforcement coming to the family home, etc.). Knowing that, you may be wondering why the subject has not yet been addressed here. Here's why:

Disclosure to children can be a complicated and fragile process; it deserves your full attention as well as that of your spouse. For this reason, we will be offering a separate guideline in the future to help you through the process of helping your children understand the situation. You may also find it helpful to have a therapist who works with the family dynamic or one who works with children to assist in this process.

Acknowledgments

ACKNOWLEDGMENTS

We would, together, like to acknowledge our esteemed colleagues who have generously read and given us feedback for our book, especially Barbara Steffens, Douglas Weiss, Milton Magness, Ken Adams, Debra Kaplan, Sheri Keffer, Jill Manning, Carol Juergensen Sheets, Laurie Hall, Pennie Carnes, Dianne Robinson, Dorit Reichental, Debra Larsen, Gaelyn Rae Emerson, and Aja Fields.

Marianne Harkin and Kimberly North, thank you for the editing and layout of our book and taking it to the next level.

To all of our clients over the years who have courageously stepped into truth by going through Full Disclosures, we honor each and every step you've taken to heal and restore after the rupture of sexual betrayal. And to all the women and men seeking and sharing truth after sexual betrayal, our hearts are with you in this process. We have the utmost respect for your courage to walk forward into truth. YOU CAN DO THIS!

From Janice:
Thank you to my family for the encouragement to follow a dream. I appreciate the sacrifices you all made as well as your belief in me. Words cannot express the gratitude I have for Aja Fields for her support, patience, and willingness to be a creative sparring partner.

Dan, who knew that the quick and simple little workbook we were going to throw together would grow into something that is so meaningful and rich for us both. Our collaboration has challenged us, deepened us, and aged us. Thank you for your patience, persistence, and clinical expertise as this grew so much bigger than we initially planned. I feel such gratitude for all I've learned from you.

These books would not have been possible without the direct influence of some special colleagues. Barbara Steffens, thank you for your passion and dedication to helping Partners heal. What a blessing your passion, dedication, and tenacity has been for our field. I would like to thank Doug Weiss for awakening therapeutic creativity in me and modeling a way to translate that into workbook exercises. I would also like to thank you for pushing me to grow beyond my comfort zone, literally pushing me at times when I needed it. APSATS community of clinicians and coaches – your passion and gracious assistance time and again when Dan and I turned to you for input is inspiring. Your DNA is stamped in many exercises in our workbooks. I would also like to acknowledge the indirect influence of Pia Mellody and Peter Levine on both the framework by which I view healing and the methods of helping it unfold.

Finally, and most importantly, thank you to all who have walked the FD path with me and taught me all that I know. I wish I knew then what I know now. My promise to you is to pass your wisdom forward to those who follow in your footsteps.

From Dan:

First and foremost, I would like to acknowledge my wife, who has championed me in this project and in my passion to work with men and women impacted by sex addiction. Thanks for always spurring me on to keep growing professionally and personally. And thank you for putting up with the many long hours that this project took to complete. I really appreciate your sacrifice so that others can be helped. You are an inspiration – I couldn't do this without you.

Janice, you are a truly gifted clinician. I'm grateful for all of your insights, and how you sharpen me to keep learning, growing, and honing. Thank you for helping me see the disclosure process in new and better ways. This workbook couldn't have come to life without you. I appreciate our collaboration!

To my amazing friends, family, and colleagues, thank you for believing in me and helping me grow into the therapist and human being that I am today. You are too many to name here, but a few who especially made this book happen: Seth, Julia, Peter, Brandi, Travis, Adam, Stephanie, Ed, Diane, Juan Carlos, Eric, Julia, Katie, Monifa, Cira, Kimberly, and all others who have been a part of helping me form Banyan Therapy Group. Thank you from the bottom of my heart.

There are many who have been trudging the road of happy destiny with me, too many to list here. But I especially want to acknowledge Sam A, RK, SC, DM, DP, SH, SGK, SL, SC, JK, JG, JL, JVS, and JH. Thank you all for helping make the promises come true for me one day at a time.

About the Authors

ABOUT THE AUTHORS

JANICE CAUDILL
PhD, CSAT-S, CCPS-S, PRT, IAT, SEP

Janice Caudill is a family psychologist in McKinney, Texas. She is a Certified Sex Addiction Therapist Supervisor, a Certified Clinical Partner Specialist Supervisor, a Certified Partner Recovery Therapist, a Partner Betrayal Therapist, Intimacy Anorexia Therapist, Somatic Experiencing Practitioner, and is EMDR trained.

Janice is the founder and clinical director of McKinney Counseling & Recovery, Intensive Recovery Healing, and Intensive Recovery Coaching. She specializes in helping individuals and couples heal from sex addiction, partner betrayal trauma, and intimacy anorexia in traditional and intensive therapy formats. The span of her professional career has focused largely on her passion for healing shock and attachment trauma in children and adults experiencing abuse, combat veterans, and those dealing the impact of other developmental or physical traumas.

www.drjanicecaudill.com

DAN DRAKE
LMFT, LPCC, CCPS-S, CSAT-S

Dan Drake is a licensed therapist in Los Angeles, California. He is a Certified Sex Addiction Therapist Supervisor, a Certified Clinical Partner Specialist, and he is EMDR trained. He has received two post doctorate degrees from Fuller Theological seminary in Marital and Family Therapy and in Theology.

Dan uses his training and specializations to treat sex addicts, their Partners, and families in his group practice. In addition to his clinical background, he has taught and spoken domestically and internationally. His passion is to help his clients restore relational, mental, emotional, physical, and spiritual wholeness to their lives.

Made in the USA
Las Vegas, NV
04 December 2023

82065341R00083